American Spirit

Student Workbook | Part 2

SpellingYouSee

Building Confidence

A Demme Learning Publication

American Spirit Student Workbook, Parts 1 and 2
©2014 Spelling You See
©2013 Karen J. Holinga, PhD
Published and distributed by Demme Learning

spellingyousee.com

1-888-854-6284 or +1 717-283-1448 | demmelearning.com
Lancaster, Pennsylvania USA

ISBN 978-1-60826-615-9 (American Spirit Student Workbook)
ISBN 978-1-60826-617-3 (Part 2)

Revision Code 1118-F

Printed in the United States of America by CJK Group
10 9 8 7 6 5 4 3 2 1

For information regarding CPSIA on this printed material call: 1-888-854-6284
and provide reference #1118-03282024

To the Instructor

This student book is the second half of Level E of Spelling You See, an innovative spelling program designed to help your student become a confident and successful speller. The first few lessons will re-introduce the letter patterns the student learned in *American Spirit Student Workbook, Part 1*. This is a good time to review the instructions and tips in your *Instructor's Handbook*.

1. Read the story to your student.

2. Read it together slowly, looking carefully at each word.

3. This lesson will review the different letter patterns that you have already learned. Today, mark <u>vowel chunks</u> in yellow, <u>consonant chunks</u> in blue, and <u>Bossy r chunks</u> in purple.

Before Helen Keller turned two, an illness made her blind and deaf. She was trapped in a dark and silent world. A teacher named Anne Sullivan came to help. Anne knew that if Helen could communicate, her life would be better. Using her fingers, Anne spelled words in Helen's palm. But Helen didn't understand. One day Anne spelled W-A-T-E-R. Helen felt water pour over her hands. Finally Helen understood! A new world was opened up to her.

Bossy r Chunks

ar   er   ir   or   ur

Vowel Chunks

aa ae ai ao au aw ay

ea ee ei eo ew ey eau

ia ie ii io iu

oa oe oi oo ou ow oy

ua ue ui uo uy

Consonant Chunks

ch gh ph sh th wh

gn kn qu wr dg ck tch

bb cc dd ff gg hh kk ll mm

nn pp rr ss tt ww vv zz

Copy the story. Mark the chunks just as you did in Section 1.

Before Helen Keller turned two,

B

an illness made her blind and

a

deaf. She was trapped in a dark

d

and silent world. A teacher named

a

Anne Sullivan came to help. Anne

A

knew that if Helen could

k

communicate, her life would be

c

better. Using her fingers, Anne

b

spelled words in Helen's palm.

s

1. Read the story to your student.

2. Read it together slowly, looking carefully at each word.

3. Together, mark **vowel chunks** in yellow, **consonant chunks** in blue, and **Bossy *r* chunks** in purple.

Before Helen Keller turned two, an illness made her blind and deaf. She was trapped in a dark and silent world. A teacher named Anne Sullivan came to help. Anne knew that if Helen could communicate, her life would be better. Using her fingers, Anne spelled words in Helen's palm. But Helen didn't understand. One day Anne spelled W-A-T-E-R. Helen felt water pour over her hands. Finally Helen understood! A new world was opened up to her.

Bossy r Chunks

ar   er   ir   or   ur

Vowel Chunks

aa   ae   ai   ao   au   aw   ay

ea   ee   ei   eo   ew   ey   eau

ia   ie   ii   io   iu

oa   oe   oi   oo   ou   ow   oy

ua   ue   ui   uo   uy

Consonant Chunks

ch   gh   ph   sh   th   wh

gn   kn   qu   wr   dg   ck   tch

bb   cc   dd   ff   gg   hh   kk   ll   mm

nn   pp   rr   ss   tt   ww   vv   zz

Copy and "chunk" the story.

Anne knew that if Helen could

A

communicate, her life would be

c

better. Using her fingers, Anne

b

spelled words in Helen's palm. But

s

Helen didn't understand. One day

H

Anne spelled W-A-T-E-R. Helen felt

A

water pour over her hands. Finally

W

Helen understood! A new world

H

was opened up to her.

W

1. Read the story to your student.

2. Read it together slowly, looking carefully at each word.

3. Together, mark <u>**vowel chunks**</u> in yellow, <u>**consonant chunks**</u> in blue, and <u>**Bossy *r* chunks**</u> in purple.

Before Helen Keller turned two, an illness made her blind and deaf. She was trapped in a dark and silent world. A teacher named Anne Sullivan came to help. Anne knew that if Helen could communicate, her life would be better. Using her fingers, Anne spelled words in Helen's palm. But Helen didn't understand. One day Anne spelled W-A-T-E-R. Helen felt water pour over her hands. Finally Helen understood! A new world was opened up to her.

Bossy r Chunks

ar   er   ir   or   ur

Vowel Chunks

aa   ae   ai   ao   au   aw   ay

ea   ee   ei   eo   ew   ey   eau

ia   ie   ii   io   iu

oa   oe   oi   oo   ou   ow   oy

ua   ue   ui   uo   uy

Consonant Chunks

ch   gh   ph   sh   th   wh

gn   kn   qu   wr   dg   ck   tch

bb   cc   dd   ff   gg   hh   kk   ll   mm

nn   pp   rr   ss   tt   ww   vv   zz

Copy and chunk the story.

Before Helen Keller turned two,

B

an illness made her blind and

a

deaf. She was trapped in a dark

d

and silent world. A teacher named

a

Anne Sullivan came to help. Anne

A

knew that if Helen could

k

communicate, her life would be

c

better. Using her fingers, Anne

b

spelled words in Helen's palm.

s

1. Read the story to your student.

2. Read it together slowly, looking carefully at each word.

3. Today, you will look for **Tricky *y* Guy**, **endings**, and **silent letters**. Mark **Tricky *y* Guy** in green, <u>endings</u> in pink or red, and <u>silent letters</u> in orange.

Before Helen Keller turned two, an illness made her blind and deaf. She was trapped in a dark and silent world. A teacher named Anne Sullivan came to help. Anne knew that if Helen could communicate, her life would be better. Using her fingers, Anne spelled words in Helen's palm. But Helen didn't understand. One day Anne spelled W-A-T-E-R. Helen felt water pour over her hands. Finally Helen understood! A new world was opened up to her.

Endings
-ed -es -ful -ing -ly

Write this week's story from dictation. Take your time and ask for help if you need it.

Before

I spelled _____ words correctly.

1. Read the story to your student.

2. Read it together slowly, looking carefully at each word.

3. Have the student mark **Tricky _y_ Guy** in green, <u>endings</u> in pink or red, and <u>silent letters</u> in orange.

Before Helen Keller turned two, an illness made her blind and deaf. She was trapped in a dark and silent world. A teacher named Anne Sullivan came to help. Anne knew that if Helen could communicate, her life would be better. Using her fingers, Anne spelled words in Helen's palm. But Helen didn't understand. One day Anne spelled W-A-T-E-R. Helen felt water pour over her hands. Finally Helen understood! A new world was opened up to her.

**Endings**
-ed -es -ful -ing -ly

Section 2: Second Dictation

See if you can write this week's story from dictation without asking for help.

I spelled _____ words correctly.

1. Read the story to your student.

2. Read it together slowly, looking carefully at each word.

3. Have the student mark <u>**vowel chunks**</u> in yellow, <u>**consonant chunks**</u> in blue, and <u>**Bossy *r* chunks**</u> in purple.

As he gulped a large breath of air, Harry knew he could do this. He was hanging upside down, his feet securely locked in place. Slowly he was lowered into a glass tank filled with water. The tank was then locked shut. The audience stared in disbelief. Harry had escaped from jail cells and locked boxes. Could he escape from this? The audience grew terrified. At last Harry Houdini emerged from the tank. The audience went wild!

Vowel Chunks

aa	ae	ai	ao	au	aw	ay
ea	ee	ei	eo	ew	ey	eau
ia	ie	ii	io	iu		
oa	oe	oi	oo	ou	ow	oy
ua	ue	ui	uo	uy		

Bossy r Chunks

ar	er	ir	or	ur

Consonant Chunks

ch	gh	ph	sh	th	wh		
gn	kn	qu	wr	dg	ck	tch	
bb	cc	dd	ff	gg	hh	kk	ll	mm
nn	pp	rr	ss	tt	ww	vv	zz

Copy and chunk the story.

As he gulped a large breath of

A

air, Harry knew he could do this.

a

He was hanging upside down, his

H

feet securely locked in place.

f

Slowly he was lowered into a

S

glass tank filled with water. The

g

tank was then locked shut. The

t

audience stared in disbelief.

a

20B

Section 1: Vowel, Consonant, and Bossy _r_ Chunks

1. Read the story to your student.

2. Read it together slowly, looking carefully at each word.

3. Have the student mark **vowel chunks** in yellow, **consonant chunks** in blue, and **Bossy _r_ chunks** in purple.

As he gulped a large breath of air, Harry knew he could do this. He was hanging upside down, his feet securely locked in place. Slowly he was lowered into a glass tank filled with water. The tank was then locked shut. The audience stared in disbelief. Harry had escaped from jail cells and locked boxes. Could he escape from this? The audience grew terrified. At last Harry Houdini emerged from the tank. The audience went wild!

Vowel Chunks

aa ae ai ao au aw ay

ea ee ei eo ew ey eau

ia ie ii io iu

oa oe oi oo ou ow oy

ua ue ui uo uy

Bossy r Chunks

ar er ir or ur

Consonant Chunks

ch gh ph sh th wh

gn kn qu wr dg ck tch

bb cc dd ff gg hh kk ll mm

nn pp rr ss tt ww vv zz

16   _American Spirit Student_

Copy and chunk the story.

The tank was then locked shut.

T

The audience stared in disbelief.

T

Harry had escaped from jail cells

H

and locked boxes. Could he escape

a

from this? The audience grew

f

terrified. At last Harry Houdini

t

emerged from the tank. The

e

audience went wild!

a

1. Read the story to your student.

2. Read it together slowly, looking carefully at each word.

3. Have the student mark <u>**vowel chunks**</u> in yellow, <u>**consonant chunks**</u> in blue, and <u>**Bossy _r_ chunks**</u> in purple.

As he gulped a large breath of air, Harry knew he could do this. He was hanging upside down, his feet securely locked in place. Slowly he was lowered into a glass tank filled with water. The tank was then locked shut. The audience stared in disbelief. Harry had escaped from jail cells and locked boxes. Could he escape from this? The audience grew terrified. At last Harry Houdini emerged from the tank. The audience went wild!

Vowel Chunks

aa ae ai ao au aw ay

ea ee ei eo ew ey eau

ia ie ii io iu

oa oe oi oo ou ow oy

ua ue ui uo uy

Bossy r Chunks

ar er ir or ur

Consonant Chunks

ch gh ph sh th wh

gn kn qu wr dg ck tch

bb cc dd ff gg hh kk ll mm

nn pp rr ss tt ww vv zz

Copy and chunk the story.

As he gulped a large breath of

A

air, Harry knew he could do this.

a

He was hanging upside down, his

H

feet securely locked in place.

f

Slowly he was lowered into a

S

glass tank filled with water. The

g

tank was then locked shut. The

t

audience stared in disbelief.

a

1. Read the story to your student.

2. Read it together slowly, looking carefully at each word.

3. Have the student mark **Tricky *y* Guy** in green, <u>endings</u> in pink or red, and <u>silent letters</u> in orange.

As he gulped a large breath of air, Harry knew he could do this. He was hanging upside down, his feet securely locked in place. Slowly he was lowered into a glass tank filled with water. The tank was then locked shut. The audience stared in disbelief. Harry had escaped from jail cells and locked boxes. Could he escape from this? The audience grew terrified. At last Harry Houdini emerged from the tank. The audience went wild!

Endings
-ed   -es   -ful   -ing   -ly

Write this week's story from dictation. Take your time and ask for help if you need it.

As

I spelled _____ words correctly.   21

1. Read the story to your student.

2. Read it together slowly, looking carefully at each word.

3. Have the student mark **Tricky *y* Guy** in green, <u>endings</u> in pink or red, and <u>silent letters</u> in orange.

As he gulped a large breath of air, Harry knew he could do this. He was hanging upside down, his feet securely locked in place. Slowly he was lowered into a glass tank filled with water. The tank was then locked shut. The audience stared in disbelief. Harry had escaped from jail cells and locked boxes. Could he escape from this? The audience grew terrified. At last Harry Houdini emerged from the tank. The audience went wild!

Endings
-ed -es -ful -ing -ly

See if you can write this week's story from dictation without asking for help.

I spelled _____ words correctly.

1. Read the story to your student.

2. Read it together slowly, looking carefully at each word.

3. Have the student mark **vowel chunks** in yellow, **consonant chunks** in blue, and **Bossy *r* chunks** in purple.

Henry Ford had built a good, solid car that people loved. But his Model T cost $850! That was more than most people could afford. He needed to cut the price without cutting quality. Then his factory started using an assembly line. As a car was built, it moved from one worker to the next. Each worker did a certain job. This saved time and money. Seven years later the Model T cost only $360.

Bossy r Chunks
ar   er   ir   or   ur

Vowel Chunks
aa   ae   ai   ao   au   aw   ay

ea   ee   ei   eo   ew   ey   eau

ia   ie   ii   io   iu

oa   oe   oi   oo   ou   ow   oy

ua   ue   ui   uo   uy

Consonant Chunks
ch   gh   ph   sh   th   wh

gn   kn   qu   wr   dg   ck   tch

bb   cc   dd   ff   gg   hh   kk   ll   mm

nn   pp   rr   ss   tt   ww   vv   zz

Section 2: Copywork

Copy and chunk the story.

Henry Ford had built a good,

H

solid car that people loved. But his

s

Model T cost $850! That was more

M

than most people could afford. He

t

needed to cut the price without

n

cutting quality. Then his factory

c

started using an assembly line. As

s

a car was built, it moved from

a

one worker to the next.

o

1. Read the story to your student.

2. Read it together slowly, looking carefully at each word.

3. Have the student mark **vowel chunks** in yellow, **consonant chunks** in blue, and **Bossy _r_ chunks** in purple.

Henry Ford had built a good, solid car that people loved. But his Model T cost $850! That was more than most people could afford. He needed to cut the price without cutting quality. Then his factory started using an assembly line. As a car was built, it moved from one worker to the next. Each worker did a certain job. This saved time and money. Seven years later the Model T cost only $360.

Bossy _r_ Chunks

ar   er   ir   or   ur

Vowel Chunks

aa   ae   ai   ao   au   aw   ay

ea   ee   ei   eo   ew   ey   eau

ia   ie   ii   io   iu

oa   oe   oi   oo   ou   ow   oy

ua   ue   ui   uo   uy

Consonant Chunks

ch   gh   ph   sh   th   wh

gn   kn   qu   wr   dg   ck   tch

bb   cc   dd   ff   gg   hh   kk   ll   mm

nn   pp   rr   ss   tt   ww   vv   zz

Section 2: Copywork

Copy and chunk the story.

He needed to cut the price

H

without cutting quality. Then his

w

factory started using an assembly

f

line. As a car was built, it moved

l

from one worker to the next. Each

f

worker did a certain job. This

w

saved time and money. Seven years

s

later the Model T cost only $360.

l

1. Read the story to your student.

2. Read it together slowly, looking carefully at each word.

3. Have the student mark **vowel chunks** in yellow, **consonant chunks** in blue, and **Bossy r chunks** in purple.

Henry Ford had built a good, solid car that people loved. But his Model T cost $850! That was more than most people could afford. He needed to cut the price without cutting quality. Then his factory started using an assembly line. As a car was built, it moved from one worker to the next. Each worker did a certain job. This saved time and money. Seven years later the Model T cost only $360.

Bossy r Chunks

ar   er   ir   or   ur

Vowel Chunks

aa ae ai ao au aw ay

ea ee ei eo ew ey eau

ia ie ii io iu

oa oe oi oo ou ow oy

ua ue ui uo uy

Consonant Chunks

ch gh ph sh th wh

gn kn qu wr dg ck tch

bb cc dd ff gg hh kk ll mm

nn pp rr ss tt ww vv zz

Copy and chunk the story.

Henry Ford had built a good,

H

solid car that people loved. But his

s

Model T cost $850! That was more

M

than most people could afford. He

t

needed to cut the price without

n

cutting quality. Then his factory

c

started using an assembly line. As

s

a car was built, it moved from

a

one worker to the next.

o

1. Read the story to your student.

2. Read it together slowly, looking carefully at each word.

3. Have the student mark **Tricky _y_ Guy** in green, <u>**endings**</u> in pink or red, and <u>**silent letters**</u> in orange.

Henry Ford had built a good, solid car that people loved. But his Model T cost $850! That was more than most people could afford. He needed to cut the price without cutting quality. Then his factory started using an assembly line. As a car was built, it moved from one worker to the next. Each worker did a certain job. This saved time and money. Seven years later the Model T cost only $360.

Endings
-ed   -es   -ful   -ing   -ly

Write this week's story from dictation. Take your time and ask for help if you need it.

Henry

I spelled _____ words correctly.

1. Read the story to your student.

2. Read it together slowly, looking carefully at each word.

3. Have the student mark <u>**Tricky _y_ Guy**</u> in green, <u>**endings**</u> in pink or red, and <u>**silent letters**</u> in orange.

Henry Ford had built a good, solid car that people loved. But his Model T cost $850! That was more than most people could afford. He needed to cut the price without cutting quality. Then his factory started using an assembly line. As a car was built, it moved from one worker to the next. Each worker did a certain job. This saved time and money. Seven years later the Model T cost only $360.

Endings
-ed   -es   -ful   -ing   -ly

See if you can write this week's story from dictation without asking for help.

I spelled _____ words correctly.

1. Read the story to your student.

2. Read it together slowly, looking carefully at each word.

3. Have the student mark **vowel chunks** in yellow, **consonant chunks** in blue, and **Bossy r chunks** in purple.

In 1920 the first American radio station went on the air. Soon there were stations across the country. They aired news and ball games. They played music and shows. In 1938 Orson Welles read a radio play called "The War of the Worlds." The story was about an attack from outer space. Before he began, he told listeners it was not real. But many people tuned in late. They thought they were hearing real news! It took quite a while to calm everyone down.

Vowel Chunks

aa ae ai ao au aw ay

ea ee ei eo ew ey eau

ia ie ii io iu

oa oe oi oo ou ow oy

ua ue ui uo uy

Consonant Chunks

ch gh ph sh th wh

gn kn qu wr dg ck tch

bb cc dd ff gg hh kk ll mm

nn pp rr ss tt ww vv zz

Bossy r Chunks

ar er ir or ur

Copy and chunk the story.

In 1920 the first American radio

I

station went on the air. Soon

s

there were stations across the

t

country. They aired news and ball

c

games. They played music and

g

shows. In 1938 Orson Welles read

s

a radio play called "The War of

a

the Worlds." The story was about

t

an attack from outer space.

a

22B

1. Read the story to your student.

2. Read it together slowly, looking carefully at each word.

3. Have the student mark <u>**vowel chunks**</u> in yellow, <u>**consonant chunks**</u> in blue, and <u>**Bossy *r* chunks**</u> in purple.

In 1920 the first American radio station went on the air. Soon there were stations across the country. They aired news and ball games. They played music and shows. In 1938 Orson Welles read a radio play called "The War of the Worlds." The story was about an attack from outer space. Before he began, he told listeners it was not real. But many people tuned in late. They thought they were hearing real news! It took quite a while to calm everyone down.

Vowel Chunks

aa ae ai ao au aw ay

ea ee ei eo ew ey eau

ia ie ii io iu

oa oe oi oo ou ow oy

ua ue ui uo uy

Consonant Chunks

ch gh ph sh th wh

gn kn qu wr dg ck tch

bb cc dd ff gg hh kk ll mm

nn pp rr ss tt ww vv zz

Bossy r Chunks

ar er ir or ur

Copy and chunk the story.

In 1938 Orson Welles read a

I

radio play called "The War of the

r

Worlds." The story was about an

W

attack from outer space. Before he

a

began, he told listeners it was not

b

real. But many people tuned in

r

late. They thought they were

l

hearing real news! It took quite

h

a while to calm everyone down.

a

1. Read the story to your student.

2. Read it together slowly, looking carefully at each word.

3. Have the student mark <u>**vowel chunks**</u> in yellow, <u>**consonant chunks**</u> in blue, and <u>**Bossy *r* chunks**</u> in purple.

In 1920 the first American radio station went on the air. Soon there were stations across the country. They aired news and ball games. They played music and shows. In 1938 Orson Welles read a radio play called "The War of the Worlds." The story was about an attack from outer space. Before he began, he told listeners it was not real. But many people tuned in late. They thought they were hearing real news! It took quite a while to calm everyone down.

Vowel Chunks

aa	ae	ai	ao	au	aw	ay
ea	ee	ei	eo	ew	ey	eau
ia	ie	ii	io	iu		
oa	oe	oi	oo	ou	ow	oy
ua	ue	ui	uo	uy		

Consonant Chunks

ch	gh	ph	sh	th	wh		
gn	kn	qu	wr	dg	ck	tch	
bb	cc	dd	ff	gg	hh	kk	ll	mm
nn	pp	rr	ss	tt	ww	vv	zz

Bossy r Chunks

ar er ir or ur

Copy and chunk the story.

In 1920 the first American radio

I

station went on the air. Soon

s

there were stations across the

t

country. They aired news and ball

c

games. They played music and

g

shows. In 1938 Orson Welles read

s

a radio play called "The War of

a

the Worlds." The story was about

t

an attack from outer space.

a

1. Read the story to your student.

2. Read it together slowly, looking carefully at each word.

3. Have the student mark **Tricky *y* Guy** in green, <u>**endings**</u> in pink or red, and <u>**silent letters**</u> in orange.

In **1920** the first American radio station went on the air. Soon there were stations across the country. They aired news and ball games. They played music and shows. In 1938 Orson Welles read a radio play called "The War of the Worlds." The story was about an attack from outer space. Before he began, he told listeners it was not real. But many people tuned in late. They thought they were hearing real news! It took quite a while to calm everyone down.

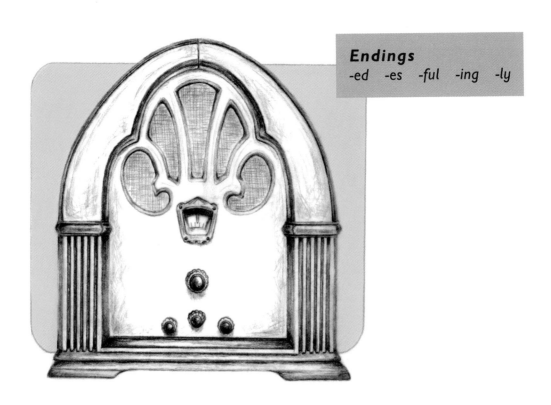

Endings
-ed   -es   -ful   -ing   -ly

Section 2: First Dictation

Write this week's story from dictation. Take your time and ask for help if you need it.

In

I spelled _____ words correctly. **41**

1. Read the story to your student.

2. Read it together slowly, looking carefully at each word.

3. Have the student mark **Tricky *y* Guy** in green, <u>**endings**</u> in pink or red, and <u>**silent letters**</u> in orange.

In 1920 the first American radio station went on the air. Soon there were stations across the country. They aired news and ball games. They played music and shows. In 1938 Orson Welles read a radio play called "The War of the Worlds." The story was about an attack from outer space. Before he began, he told listeners it was not real. But many people tuned in late. They thought they were hearing real news! It took quite a while to calm everyone down.

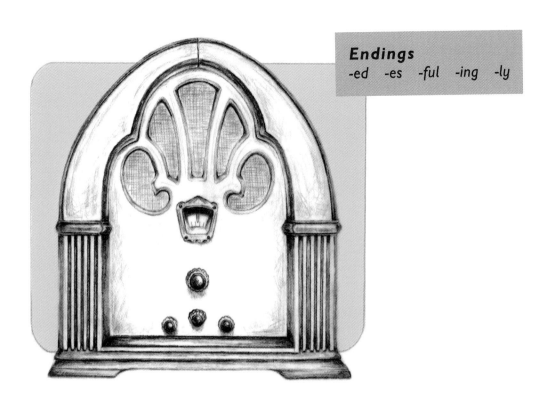

Endings
-ed   -es   -ful   -ing   -ly

Section 2: Second Dictation

See if you can write this week's story from dictation without asking for help.

I spelled _____ words correctly.   43

1. Read the story to your student.

2. Read it together slowly, looking carefully at each word.

3. Have the student mark **vowel chunks** in yellow, **consonant chunks** in blue, and **Bossy *r* chunks** in purple.

Farmers in the Great Plains plowed the native grasslands to plant wheat. They did not know the grass kept the soil healthy and in place. For eight years, there was not enough rain. Nothing grew. The dry soil became like powder. Strong winds blew the soil away in massive dust storms. People called the storms "black blizzards." During the Dust Bowl of the 1930s, many families left the plains to find hope elsewhere.

Vowel Chunks

aa   ae   ai   ao   au   aw   ay

ea   ee   ei   eo   ew   ey   eau

ia   ie   ii   io   iu

oa   oe   oi   oo   ou   ow   oy

ua   ue   ui   uo   uy

Consonant Chunks

ch   gh   ph   sh   th   wh

gn   kn   qu   wr   dg   ck   tch

bb   cc   dd   ff   gg   hh   kk   ll   mm

nn   pp   rr   ss   tt   ww   vv   zz

Bossy r Chunks

ar   er   ir   or   ur

Copy and chunk the story.

Farmers in the Great Plains

F

plowed the native grasslands to

P

plant wheat. They did not know

P

the grass kept the soil healthy and

t

in place. For eight years, there

i

was not enough rain. Nothing

w

grew. The dry soil became like

g

powder. Strong winds blew the

P

soil away in massive dust storms.

s

23B

1. Read the story to your student.

2. Read it together slowly, looking carefully at each word.

3. Have the student mark **vowel chunks** in yellow, **consonant chunks** in blue, and **Bossy *r* chunks** in purple.

Farmers in the Great Plains plowed the native grasslands to plant wheat. They did not know the grass kept the soil healthy and in place. For eight years, there was not enough rain. Nothing grew. The dry soil became like powder. Strong winds blew the soil away in massive dust storms. People called the storms "black blizzards." During the Dust Bowl of the 1930s, many families left the plains to find hope elsewhere.

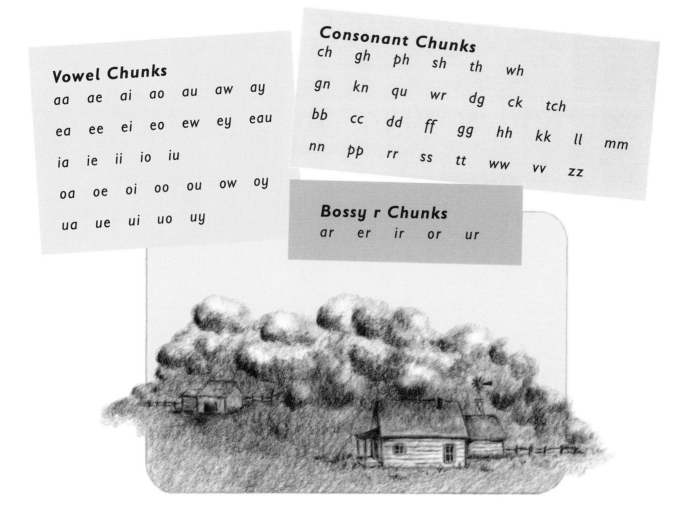

Vowel Chunks

aa ae ai ao au aw ay

ea ee ei eo ew ey eau

ia ie ii io iu

oa oe oi oo ou ow oy

ua ue ui uo uy

Consonant Chunks

ch gh ph sh th wh

gn kn qu wr dg ck tch

bb cc dd ff gg hh kk ll mm

nn pp rr ss tt ww vv zz

Bossy r Chunks

ar er ir or ur

Copy and chunk the story.

For eight years, there was not

F

enough rain. Nothing grew. The

e

dry soil became like powder.

d

Strong winds blew the soil away

S

in massive dust storms. People

i

called the storms "black blizzards."

c

During the Dust Bowl of the

D

1930s, many families left the plains

1

to find hope elsewhere.

t

1. Read the story to your student.

2. Read it together slowly, looking carefully at each word.

3. Have the student mark <u>**vowel chunks**</u> in yellow, <u>**consonant chunks**</u> in blue, and <u>**Bossy *r* chunks**</u> in purple.

Farmers in the Great Plains plowed the native grasslands to plant wheat. They did not know the grass kept the soil healthy and in place. For eight years, there was not enough rain. Nothing grew. The dry soil became like powder. Strong winds blew the soil away in massive dust storms. People called the storms "black blizzards." During the Dust Bowl of the 1930s, many families left the plains to find hope elsewhere.

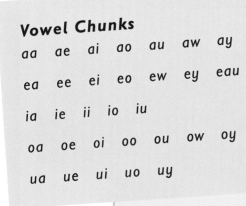

Vowel Chunks

aa ae ai ao au aw ay

ea ee ei eo ew ey eau

ia ie ii io iu

oa oe oi oo ou ow oy

ua ue ui uo uy

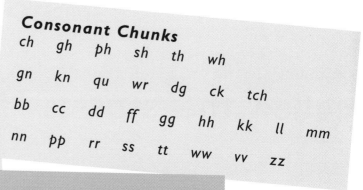

Consonant Chunks

ch gh ph sh th wh

gn kn qu wr dg ck tch

bb cc dd ff gg hh kk ll mm

nn pp rr ss tt ww vv zz

Bossy r Chunks

ar er ir or ur

Copy and chunk the story.

Farmers in the Great Plains

F

plowed the native grasslands to

p

plant wheat. They did not know

p

the grass kept the soil healthy and

t

in place. For eight years, there

i

was not enough rain. Nothing

w

grew. The dry soil became like

g

powder. Strong winds blew the

p

soil away in massive dust storms.

s

1. Read the story to your student.

2. Read it together slowly, looking carefully at each word.

3. Have the student mark **Tricky *y* Guy** in green, <u>endings</u> in pink or red, and <u>silent letters</u> in orange.

Farmers in the Great Plains plowed the native grasslands to plant wheat. They did not know the grass kept the soil healthy and in place. For eight years, there was not enough rain. Nothing grew. The dry soil became like powder. Strong winds blew the soil away in massive dust storms. People called the storms "black blizzards." During the Dust Bowl of the 1930s, many families left the plains to find hope elsewhere.

Endings
-ed   -es   -ful   -ing   -ly

Write this week's story from dictation. Take your time and ask for help if you need it.

Farmers

I spelled _____ words correctly.

1. Read the story to your student.

2. Read it together slowly, looking carefully at each word.

3. Have the student mark **Tricky _y_ Guy** in green, **endings** in pink or red, and **silent letters** in orange.

Farmers in the Great Plains plowed the native grasslands to plant wheat. They did not know the grass kept the soil healthy and in place. For eight years, there was not enough rain. Nothing grew. The dry soil became like powder. Strong winds blew the soil away in massive dust storms. People called the storms "black blizzards." During the Dust Bowl of the 1930s, many families left the plains to find hope elsewhere.

Endings
-ed   -es   -ful   -ing   -ly

Section 2: Second Dictation

See if you can write this week's story from dictation without asking for help.

I spelled _____ words correctly.

1. Read the story to your student.

2. Read it together slowly, looking carefully at each word.

3. Have the student mark <u>**vowel chunks**</u> in yellow, <u>**consonant chunks**</u> in blue, and <u>**Bossy *r* chunks**</u> in purple.

Mr. Wright wound the long rubber band. When he let go, the light wooden toy flew across the room. Orville and Wilbur stared in wonder. They played with the toy until it broke. Then they made their own. The toy sparked a lifelong interest in flying machines. Over the years, they built, tested, and modified many machines. In 1903, the Wright brothers took turns flying the first successful airplane. They didn't fly very far or high, but they flew!

Bossy r Chunks

ar   er   ir   or   ur

Vowel Chunks

aa   ae   ai   ao   au   aw   ay

ea   ee   ei   eo   ew   ey   eau

ia   ie   ii   io   iu

oa   oe   oi   oo   ou   ow   oy

ua   ue   ui   uo   uy

Consonant Chunks

ch   gh   ph   sh   th   wh

gn   kn   qu   wr   dg   ck   tch

bb   cc   dd   ff   gg   hh   kk   ll   mm

nn   pp   rr   ss   tt   ww   vv   zz

Copy and chunk the story.

Mr. Wright wound the long

M

rubber band. When he let go, the

r

light wooden toy flew across the

l

room. Orville and Wilbur stared

r

in wonder. They played with the

i

toy until it broke. Then they made

t

their own. The toy sparked a

t

lifelong interest in flying machines.

l

24B

1. Read the story to your student.

2. Read it together slowly, looking carefully at each word.

3. Have the student mark **vowel chunks** in yellow, **consonant chunks** in blue, and **Bossy *r* chunks** in purple.

Mr. Wright wound the long rubber band. When he let go, the light wooden toy flew across the room. Orville and Wilbur stared in wonder. They played with the toy until it broke. Then they made their own. The toy sparked a lifelong interest in flying machines. Over the years, they built, tested, and modified many machines. In 1903, the Wright brothers took turns flying the first successful airplane. They didn't fly very far or high, but they flew!

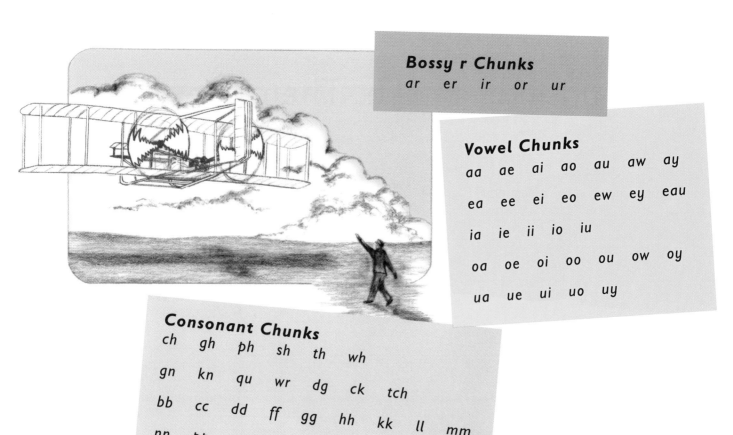

Bossy r Chunks

ar   er   ir   or   ur

Vowel Chunks

aa   ae   ai   ao   au   aw   ay

ea   ee   ei   eo   ew   ey   eau

ia   ie   ii   io   iu

oa   oe   oi   oo   ou   ow   oy

ua   ue   ui   uo   uy

Consonant Chunks

ch   gh   ph   sh   th   wh

gn   kn   qu   wr   dg   ck   tch

bb   cc   dd   ff   gg   hh   kk   ll   mm

nn   pp   rr   ss   tt   ww   vv   zz

Copy and chunk the story.

Then they made their own. The
T

toy sparked a lifelong interest
t

in flying machines. Over the years,
i

they built, tested, and modified
t

many machines. In 1903, the
m

Wright brothers took turns flying
W

the first successful airplane. They
t

didn't fly very far or high, but
d

they flew!
t

1. Read the story to your student.

2. Read it together slowly, looking carefully at each word.

3. Have the student mark <u>**vowel chunks**</u> in yellow, <u>**consonant chunks**</u> in blue, and <u>**Bossy *r* chunks**</u> in purple.

Mr. Wright wound the long rubber band. When he let go, the light wooden toy flew across the room. Orville and Wilbur stared in wonder. They played with the toy until it broke. Then they made their own. The toy sparked a lifelong interest in flying machines. Over the years, they built, tested, and modified many machines. In 1903, the Wright brothers took turns flying the first successful airplane. They didn't fly very far or high, but they flew!

Bossy r Chunks

ar   er   ir   or   ur

Vowel Chunks

aa   ae   ai   ao   au   aw   ay

ea   ee   ei   eo   ew   ey   eau

ia   ie   ii   io   iu

oa   oe   oi   oo   ou   ow   oy

ua   ue   ui   uo   uy

Consonant Chunks

ch   gh   ph   sh   th   wh

gn   kn   qu   wr   dg   ck   tch

bb   cc   dd   ff   gg   hh   kk   ll   mm

nn   pp   rr   ss   tt   ww   vv   zz

Copy and chunk the story.

Mr. Wright wound the long

M

rubber band. When he let go, the

r

light wooden toy flew across the

l

room. Orville and Wilbur stared

r

in wonder. They played with the

i

toy until it broke. Then they made

t

their own. The toy sparked a

t

lifelong interest in flying machines.

l

24D

Section 1: Tricky *y* Guy, Endings, Silent Letters

1. Read the story to your student.

2. Read it together slowly, looking carefully at each word.

3. Have the student mark **Tricky *y* Guy** in green, <u>**endings**</u> in pink or red, and <u>**silent letters**</u> in orange.

Mr. Wright wound the long rubber band. When he let go, the light wooden toy flew across the room. Orville and Wilbur stared in wonder. They played with the toy until it broke. Then they made their own. The toy sparked a lifelong interest in flying machines. Over the years, they built, tested, and modified many machines. In 1903, the Wright brothers took turns flying the first successful airplane. They didn't fly very far or high, but they flew!

Endings
-ed -es -ful -ing -ly

Section 2: First Dictation

Write this week's story from dictation. Take your time and ask for help if you need it.

Mr.

I spelled _____ words correctly.

1. Read the story to your student.

2. Read it together slowly, looking carefully at each word.

3. Have the student mark **Tricky _y_ Guy** in green, <u>**endings**</u> in pink or red, and <u>**silent letters**</u> in orange.

Mr. Wright wound the long rubber band. When he let go, the light wooden toy flew across the room. Orville and Wilbur stared in wonder. They played with the toy until it broke. Then they made their own. The toy sparked a lifelong interest in flying machines. Over the years, they built, tested, and modified many machines. In 1903, the Wright brothers took turns flying the first successful airplane. They didn't fly very far or high, but they flew!

Endings
-ed   -es   -ful   -ing   -ly

Section 2: Second Dictation

See if you can write this week's story from dictation without asking for help.

I spelled _____ words correctly.

1. Read the story to your student.

2. Read it together slowly, looking carefully at each word.

3. This week you and your student will be looking for and marking all six letter patterns that you have learned. They are **vowel chunks** (yellow), **consonant chunks** (blue), **Bossy *r* chunks** (purple), **Tricky *y* Guy** (green), **endings** (pink or red), and **silent letters** (orange).

Amelia wasn't afraid to try new things. She had the courage to act on her dreams. She was the first woman pilot to fly across the Atlantic Ocean by herself. Then she tried to be the first to fly around the world. She took one person with her. Something went very wrong on that trip. No one ever found Amelia, her friend, or the plane. In her short life, Amelia Earhart inspired many women to follow their dreams.

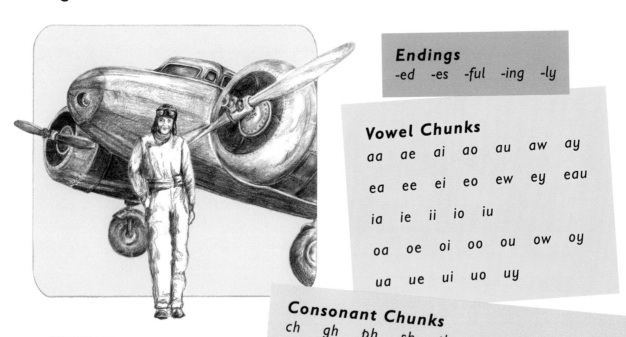

Endings
-ed   -es   -ful   -ing   -ly

Vowel Chunks
aa   ae   ai   ao   au   aw   ay
ea   ee   ei   eo   ew   ey   eau
ia   ie   ii   io   iu
oa   oe   oi   oo   ou   ow   oy
ua   ue   ui   uo   uy

Consonant Chunks
ch   gh   ph   sh   th   wh
gn   kn   qu   wr   dg   ck   tch
bb   cc   dd   ff   gg   hh   kk   ll   mm
nn   pp   rr   ss   tt   ww   vv   zz

Bossy r Chunks
ar   er   ir   or   ur

Copy and chunk the story.

Amelia wasn't afraid to try new

A

things. She had the courage to act

t

on her dreams. She was the first

o

woman pilot to fly across the

w

Atlantic Ocean by herself. Then

A

she tried to be the first to fly

s

around the world. She took one

a

person with her. Something went

P

very wrong on that trip.

v

1. Read the story to your student.

2. Read it together slowly, looking carefully at each word.

3. Have the student mark the **vowel chunks** (yellow), **consonant chunks** (blue), **Bossy _r_ chunks** (purple), **Tricky _y_ Guy** (green), **endings** (pink or red), and **silent letters** (orange).

Amelia wasn't afraid to try new things. She had the courage to act on her dreams. She was the first woman pilot to fly across the Atlantic Ocean by herself. Then she tried to be the first to fly around the world. She took one person with her. Something went very wrong on that trip. No one ever found Amelia, her friend, or the plane. In her short life, Amelia Earhart inspired many women to follow their dreams.

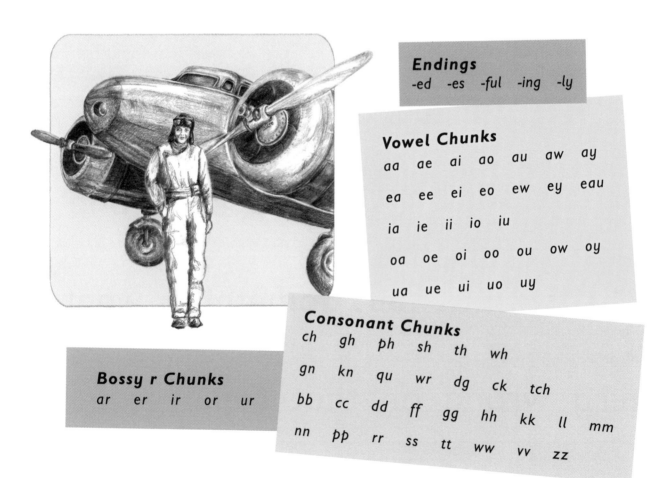

Endings
-ed -es -ful -ing -ly

Vowel Chunks
aa ae ai ao au aw ay
ea ee ei eo ew ey eau
ia ie ii io iu
oa oe oi oo ou ow oy
ua ue ui uo uy

Consonant Chunks
ch gh ph sh th wh
gn kn qu wr dg ck tch
bb cc dd ff gg hh kk ll mm
nn pp rr ss tt ww vv zz

Bossy r Chunks
ar er ir or ur

Copy and chunk the story.

Then she tried to be the first to

T

fly around the world. She took

f

one person with her. Something

o

went very wrong on that trip.

w

No one ever found Amelia, her

N

friend, or the plane. In her short

f

life, Amelia Earhart inspired many

l

women to follow their dreams.

w

1. Read the story to your student.

2. Read it together slowly, looking carefully at each word.

3. Have the student mark the <u>**vowel chunks**</u> (yellow), <u>**consonant chunks**</u> (blue), <u>**Bossy *r* chunks**</u> (purple), <u>**Tricky *y* Guy**</u> (green), <u>**endings**</u> (pink or red), and <u>**silent letters**</u> (orange).

Amelia wasn't afraid to try new things. She had the courage to act on her dreams. She was the first woman pilot to fly across the Atlantic Ocean by herself. Then she tried to be the first to fly around the world. She took one person with her. Something went very wrong on that trip. No one ever found Amelia, her friend, or the plane. In her short life, Amelia Earhart inspired many women to follow their dreams.

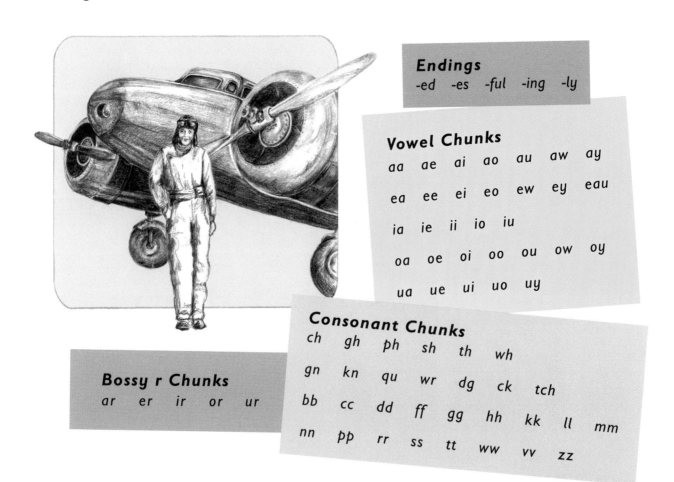

Endings
-ed   -es   -ful   -ing   -ly

Vowel Chunks
aa   ae   ai   ao   au   aw   ay
ea   ee   ei   eo   ew   ey   eau
ia   ie   ii   io   iu
oa   oe   oi   oo   ou   ow   oy
ua   ue   ui   uo   uy

Consonant Chunks
ch   gh   ph   sh   th   wh
gn   kn   qu   wr   dg   ck   tch
bb   cc   dd   ff   gg   hh   kk   ll   mm
nn   pp   rr   ss   tt   ww   vv   zz

Bossy r Chunks
ar   er   ir   or   ur

Copy and chunk the story.

Amelia wasn't afraid to try new

A

things. She had the courage to act

t

on her dreams. She was the first

o

woman pilot to fly across the

w

Atlantic Ocean by herself. Then

A

she tried to be the first to fly

s

around the world. She took one

a

person with her. Something went

P

very wrong on that trip.

V

1. Read the story to your student.

2. Read it together slowly, looking carefully at each word.

3. Have the student mark the <u>vowel chunks</u> (yellow), **consonant chunks** (blue), **Bossy *r* chunks** (purple), **Tricky *y* Guy** (green), <u>endings</u> (pink or red), and <u>silent letters</u> (orange).

Amelia wasn't afraid to try new things. She had the courage to act on her dreams. She was the first woman pilot to fly across the Atlantic Ocean by herself. Then she tried to be the first to fly around the world. She took one person with her. Something went very wrong on that trip. No one ever found Amelia, her friend, or the plane. In her short life, Amelia Earhart inspired many women to follow their dreams.

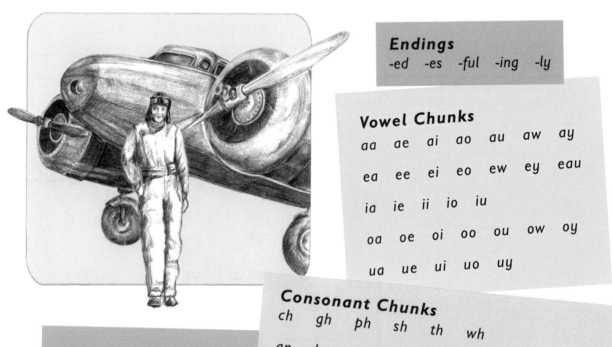

Endings
-ed -es -ful -ing -ly

Vowel Chunks
aa ae ai ao au aw ay
ea ee ei eo ew ey eau
ia ie ii io iu
oa oe oi oo ou ow oy
ua ue ui uo uy

Consonant Chunks
ch gh ph sh th wh
gn kn qu wr dg ck tch
bb cc dd ff gg hh kk ll mm
nn pp rr ss tt ww vv zz

Bossy r Chunks
ar er ir or ur

Section 2: First Dictation

Write this week's story from dictation. Take your time and ask for help if you need it.

Amelia

I spelled _____ words correctly.

1. Read the story to your student.

2. Read it together slowly, looking carefully at each word.

3. Have the student mark the <u>**vowel chunks**</u> (yellow), <u>**consonant chunks**</u> (blue), <u>**Bossy *r* chunks**</u> (purple), <u>**Tricky *y* Guy**</u> (green), <u>**endings**</u> (pink or red), and <u>**silent letters**</u> (orange).

Amelia wasn't afraid to try new things. She had the courage to act on her dreams. She was the first woman pilot to fly across the Atlantic Ocean by herself. Then she tried to be the first to fly around the world. She took one person with her. Something went very wrong on that trip. No one ever found Amelia, her friend, or the plane. In her short life, Amelia Earhart inspired many women to follow their dreams.

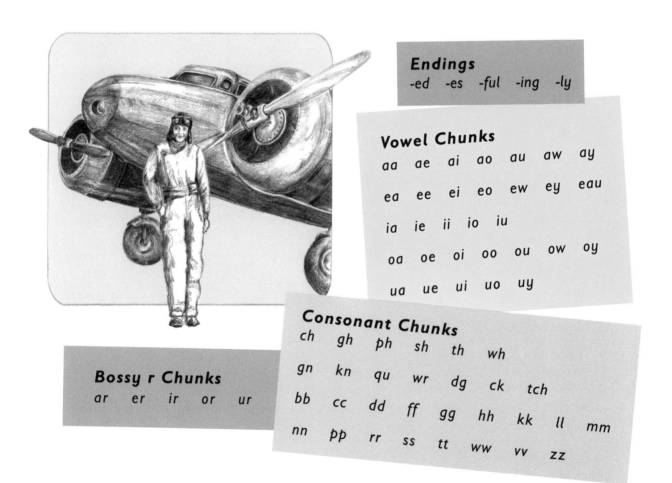

Endings
-ed -es -ful -ing -ly

Vowel Chunks
aa ae ai ao au aw ay
ea ee ei eo ew ey eau
ia ie ii io iu
oa oe oi oo ou ow oy
ua ue ui uo uy

Consonant Chunks
ch gh ph sh th wh
gn kn qu wr dg ck tch
bb cc dd ff gg hh kk ll mm
nn pp rr ss tt ww vv zz

Bossy r Chunks
ar er ir or ur

Section 2: Second Dictation

See if you can write this week's story from dictation without asking for help.

I spelled _____ words correctly.   **73**

1. Read the story to your student.

2. Read it together slowly, looking carefully at each word.

3. This week you and your student will be looking for and marking all six letter patterns that you have learned. They are **vowel chunks** (yellow), **consonant chunks** (blue), **Bossy *r* chunks** (purple), **Tricky *y* Guy** (green), **endings** (pink or red), and **silent letters** (orange).

In John F. Kennedy's first speech as president, he challenged Americans. He said, "Ask not what your country can do for you. Ask what you can do for your country." He thought it would be good for America if young people helped in other countries. Many young Americans agreed and joined the Peace Corps. They went and served all over the world.

Bossy r Chunks

ar   er   ir   or   ur

Vowel Chunks

aa	ae	ai	ao	au	aw	ay
ea	ee	ei	eo	ew	ey	eau
ia	ie	ii	io	iu		
oa	oe	oi	oo	ou	ow	oy
ua	ue	ui	uo	uy		

Endings

-ed   -es   -ful   -ing   -ly

Consonant Chunks

ch	gh	ph	sh	th	wh		
gn	kn	qu	wr	dg	ck	tch	
bb	cc	dd	ff	gg	hh	kk	ll	mm
nn	pp	rr	ss	tt	ww	vv	zz

Copy and chunk the story.

In John F. Kennedy's first speech

I

as president, he challenged

a

Americans. He said, "Ask not what

A

your country can do for you. Ask

y

what you can do for your

w

country." He thought it would be

c

good for America if young people

g

helped in other countries.

h

1. Read the story to your student.

2. Read it together slowly, looking carefully at each word.

3. Have the student mark the **vowel chunks** (yellow), **consonant chunks** (blue), **Bossy _r_ chunks** (purple), **Tricky _y_ Guy** (green), **endings** (pink or red), and **silent letters** (orange).

In John F. Kennedy's first speech as president, he challenged Americans. He said, "Ask not what your country can do for you. Ask what you can do for your country." He thought it would be good for America if young people helped in other countries. Many young Americans agreed and joined the Peace Corps. They went and served all over the world.

Bossy r Chunks
ar   er   ir   or   ur

Vowel Chunks
aa   ae   ai   ao   au   aw   ay
ea   ee   ei   eo   ew   ey   eau
ia   ie   ii   io   iu
oa   oe   oi   oo   ou   ow   oy
ua   ue   ui   uo   uy

Endings
-ed   -es   -ful   -ing   -ly

Consonant Chunks
ch   gh   ph   sh   th   wh
gn   kn   qu   wr   dg   ck   tch
bb   cc   dd   ff   gg   hh   kk   ll   mm
nn   pp   rr   ss   tt   ww   vv   zz

Copy and chunk the story.

He said, "Ask not what your

H

country can do for you. Ask what

c

you can do for your country." He

y

thought it would be good for

t

America if young people helped in

A

other countries. Many young

o

Americans agreed and joined the

A

Peace Corps. They went and served

P

all over the world.

a

26C

Section 1: All Letter Patterns

1. Read the story to your student.

2. Read it together slowly, looking carefully at each word.

3. Have the student mark the <u>vowel chunks</u> (yellow), <u>consonant chunks</u> (blue), <u>Bossy *r* chunks</u> (purple), <u>Tricky *y* Guy</u> (green), <u>endings</u> (pink or red), and <u>silent letters</u> (orange).

In John F. Kennedy's first speech as president, he challenged Americans. He said, "Ask not what your country can do for you. Ask what you can do for your country." He thought it would be good for America if young people helped in other countries. Many young Americans agreed and joined the Peace Corps. They went and served all over the world.

Bossy r Chunks

ar   er   ir   or   ur

Vowel Chunks

aa ae ai ao au aw ay

ea ee ei eo ew ey eau

ia ie ii io iu

oa oe oi oo ou ow oy

ua ue ui uo uy

Endings

-ed -es -ful -ing -ly

Consonant Chunks

ch gh ph sh th wh

gn kn qu wr dg ck tch

bb cc dd ff gg hh kk ll mm

nn pp rr ss tt ww vv zz

Copy and chunk the story.

In John F. Kennedy's first speech

I

as president, he challenged

a

Americans. He said, "Ask not what

A

your country can do for you. Ask

y

what you can do for your

w

country." He thought it would be

c

good for America if young people

g

helped in other countries.

h

1. Read the story to your student.

2. Read it together slowly, looking carefully at each word.

3. Have the student mark the <u>**vowel chunks**</u> (yellow), <u>**consonant chunks**</u> (blue), <u>**Bossy *r* chunks**</u> (purple), <u>**Tricky *y* Guy**</u> (green), <u>**endings**</u> (pink or red), and <u>**silent letters**</u> (orange).

In John F. Kennedy's first speech as president, he challenged Americans. He said, "Ask not what your country can do for you. Ask what you can do for your country." He thought it would be good for America if young people helped in other countries. Many young Americans agreed and joined the Peace Corps. They went and served all over the world.

Bossy r Chunks

ar   er   ir   or   ur

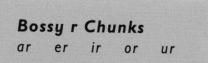

Vowel Chunks

aa   ae   ai   ao   au   aw   ay

ea   ee   ei   eo   ew   ey   eau

ia   ie   ii   io   iu

oa   oe   oi   oo   ou   ow   oy

ua   ue   ui   uo   uy

Endings

-ed -es -ful -ing -ly

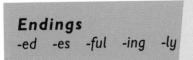

Consonant Chunks

ch   gh   ph   sh   th   wh

gn   kn   qu   wr   dg   ck   tch

bb   cc   dd   ff   gg   hh   kk   ll   mm

nn   pp   rr   ss   tt   ww   vv   zz

Write this week's story from dictation. Take your time and ask for help if you need it.

In

I spelled _____ words correctly.

1. Read the story to your student.

2. Read it together slowly, looking carefully at each word.

3. Have the student mark the **vowel chunks** (yellow), **consonant chunks** (blue), **Bossy *r* chunks** (purple), **Tricky *y* Guy** (green), **endings** (pink or red), and **silent letters** (orange).

In John F. Kennedy's first speech as president, he challenged Americans. He said, "Ask not what your country can do for you. Ask what you can do for your country." He thought it would be good for America if young people helped in other countries. Many young Americans agreed and joined the Peace Corps. They went and served all over the world.

Bossy r Chunks

ar   er   ir   or   ur

Vowel Chunks

aa ae ai ao au aw ay

ea ee ei eo ew ey eau

ia ie ii io iu

oa oe oi oo ou ow oy

ua ue ui uo uy

Endings

-ed   -es   -ful   -ing   -ly

Consonant Chunks

ch gh ph sh th wh

gn kn qu wr dg ck tch

bb cc dd ff gg hh kk ll mm

nn pp rr ss tt ww vv zz

Section 2: Second Dictation

See if you can write this week's story from dictation without asking for help.

27A

Section 1: All Letter Patterns

1. Read the story to your student.

2. Read it together slowly, looking carefully at each word.

3. This week you and your student will be looking for and marking all six letter patterns that you have learned. They are **vowel chunks** (yellow), **consonant chunks** (blue), **Bossy *r* chunks** (purple), **Tricky *y* Guy** (green), **endings** (pink or red), and **silent letters** (orange). See the *Handbook* for tips on marking overlapping chunks.

As a girl, Sally loved science. She also loved being outdoors and active. For years Sally played tennis. She was very good. She even thought about playing tennis for a career. Instead she decided to go to college. She studied physics and English. In time, all her hard work paid off. So did her physical fitness. In 1983 Sally Ride became the first American woman in space.

Vowel Chunks

aa ae ai ao au aw ay

ea ee ei eo ew ey eau

ia ie ii io iu

oa oe oi oo ou ow oy

ua ue ui uo uy

Endings
-ed -es -ful -ing -ly

Consonant Chunks

ch gh ph sh th wh

gn kn qu wr dg ck tch

bb cc dd ff gg hh kk ll mm

nn pp rr ss tt ww vv zz

Bossy r Chunks
ar er ir or ur

American Spirit Student

Copy and chunk the story.

As a girl, Sally loved science. She
A

also loved being outdoors and
a

active. For years Sally played
a

tennis. She was very good. She
t

even thought about playing tennis
e

for a career. Instead she decided
f

to go to college. She studied
t

physics and English. In time, all her
p

hard work paid off.
h

1. Read the story to your student.

2. Read it together slowly, looking carefully at each word.

3. Have the student mark the **vowel chunks** (yellow), **consonant chunks** (blue), **Bossy _r_ chunks** (purple), **Tricky _y_ Guy** (green), **endings** (pink or red), and **silent letters** (orange).

As a girl, Sally loved science. She also loved being outdoors and active. For years Sally played tennis. She was very good. She even thought about playing tennis for a career. Instead she decided to go to college. She studied physics and English. In time, all her hard work paid off. So did her physical fitness. In 1983 Sally Ride became the first American woman in space.

Vowel Chunks

aa ae ai ao au aw ay

ea ee ei eo ew ey eau

ia ie ii io iu

oa oe oi oo ou ow oy

ua ue ui uo uy

Endings

-ed -es -ful -ing -ly

Consonant Chunks

ch gh ph sh th wh

gn kn qu wr dg ck tch

bb cc dd ff gg hh kk ll mm

nn pp rr ss tt ww vv zz

Bossy r Chunks

ar er ir or ur

Copy and chunk the story.

For years Sally played tennis. She

F

was very good. She even thought

w

about playing tennis for a career.

a

Instead she decided to go to

I

college. She studied physics and

c

English. In time, all her hard work

E

paid off. So did her physical

P

fitness. In 1983 Sally Ride became

f

the first American woman in space.

t

1. Read the story to your student.

2. Read it together slowly, looking carefully at each word.

3. Have the student mark the **vowel chunks** (yellow), **consonant chunks** (blue), **Bossy _r_ chunks** (purple), **Tricky _y_ Guy** (green), **endings** (pink or red), and **silent letters** (orange).

As a girl, Sally loved science. She also loved being outdoors and active. For years Sally played tennis. She was very good. She even thought about playing tennis for a career. Instead she decided to go to college. She studied physics and English. In time, all her hard work paid off. So did her physical fitness. In 1983 Sally Ride became the first American woman in space.

Vowel Chunks

aa   ae   ai   ao   au   aw   ay

ea   ee   ei   eo   ew   ey   eau

ia   ie   ii   io   iu

oa   oe   oi   oo   ou   ow   oy

ua   ue   ui   uo   uy

Endings
-ed   -es   -ful   -ing   -ly

Consonant Chunks

ch   gh   ph   sh   th   wh

gn   kn   qu   wr   dg   ck   tch

bb   cc   dd   ff   gg   hh   kk   ll   mm

nn   pp   rr   ss   tt   ww   vv   zz

Bossy r Chunks

ar   er   ir   or   ur

Copy and chunk the story.

As a girl, Sally loved science. She

A

also loved being outdoors and

a

active. For years Sally played

a

tennis. She was very good. She

t

even thought about playing tennis

e

for a career. Instead she decided

f

to go to college. She studied

t

physics and English. In time, all her

p

hard work paid off.

h

1. Read the story to your student.

2. Read it together slowly, looking carefully at each word.

3. Have the student mark the **vowel chunks** (yellow), **consonant chunks** (blue), **Bossy *r* chunks** (purple), **Tricky *y* Guy** (green), **endings** (pink or red), and **silent letters** (orange).

As a girl, Sally loved science. She also loved being outdoors and active. For years Sally played tennis. She was very good. She even thought about playing tennis for a career. Instead she decided to go to college. She studied physics and English. In time, all her hard work paid off. So did her physical fitness. In 1983 Sally Ride became the first American woman in space.

Vowel Chunks

aa	ae	ai	ao	au	aw	ay
ea	ee	ei	eo	ew	ey	eau
ia	ie	ii	io	iu		
oa	oe	oi	oo	ou	ow	oy
ua	ue	ui	uo	uy		

Endings

-ed   -es   -ful   -ing   -ly

Consonant Chunks

ch	gh	ph	sh	th	wh		
gn	kn	qu	wr	dg	ck	tch	
bb	cc	dd	ff	gg	hh	kk	ll	mm
nn	pp	rr	ss	tt	ww	vv	zz	

Bossy r Chunks

ar   er   ir   or   ur

Section 2: First Dictation

Write this week's story from dictation. Take your time and ask for help if you
need it.

As

1. Read the story to your student.

2. Read it together slowly, looking carefully at each word.

3. Have the student mark the **vowel chunks** (yellow), **consonant chunks** (blue), **Bossy *r* chunks** (purple), **Tricky *y* Guy** (green), **endings** (pink or red), and **silent letters** (orange).

As a girl, Sally loved science. She also loved being outdoors and active. For years Sally played tennis. She was very good. She even thought about playing tennis for a career. Instead she decided to go to college. She studied physics and English. In time, all her hard work paid off. So did her physical fitness. In 1983 Sally Ride became the first American woman in space.

Vowel Chunks

aa   ae   ai   ao   au   aw   ay

ea   ee   ei   eo   ew   ey   eau

ia   ie   ii   io   iu

oa   oe   oi   oo   ou   ow   oy

ua   ue   ui   uo   uy

Endings

-ed   -es   -ful   -ing   -ly

Consonant Chunks

ch   gh   ph   sh   th   wh

gn   kn   qu   wr   dg   ck   tch

bb   cc   dd   ff   gg   hh   kk   ll   mm

nn   pp   rr   ss   tt   ww   vv   zz

Bossy r Chunks

ar   er   ir   or   ur

Section 2: Second Dictation

See if you can write this week's story from dictation without asking for help.

I spelled _____ words correctly.

1. Read the story to your student.

2. Read it together slowly, looking carefully at each word.

3. This week you and your student will be looking for and marking all six letter patterns that you have learned. They are **vowel chunks** (yellow), **consonant chunks** (blue), **Bossy *r* chunks** (purple), **Tricky *y* Guy** (green), **endings** (pink or red), and **silent letters** (orange).

Philo was very interested in electronics. When he was a teenager, he found a stash of science magazines. He studied them carefully. He learned that scientists were trying to make a new machine. It would use electricity to send and show pictures. He thought about it. He talked with his science teachers. One day he drew a picture on the chalkboard. It showed how a television could work. Philo Farnsworth's plan was the first idea that worked.

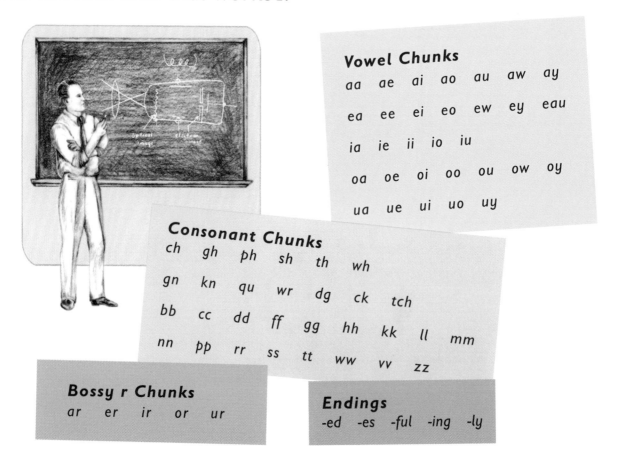

Vowel Chunks

aa ae ai ao au aw ay
ea ee ei eo ew ey eau
ia ie ii io iu
oa oe oi oo ou ow oy
ua ue ui uo uy

Consonant Chunks

ch gh ph sh th wh
gn kn qu wr dg ck tch
bb cc dd ff gg hh kk ll mm
nn pp rr ss tt ww vv zz

Bossy r Chunks
ar er ir or ur

Endings
-ed -es -ful -ing -ly

Copy and chunk the story.

Philo was very interested in

P

electronics. When he was a

e

teenager, he found a stash of

t

science magazines. He studied

s

them carefully. He learned that

t

scientists were trying to make a

s

new machine. It would use

n

electricity to send and show

e

pictures. He thought about it.

P

1. Read the story to your student.

2. Read it together slowly, looking carefully at each word.

3. Have the student mark the **vowel chunks** (yellow), **consonant chunks** (blue), **Bossy _r_ chunks** (purple), **Tricky _y_ Guy** (green), **endings** (pink or red), and **silent letters** (orange).

Philo was very interested in electronics. When he was a teenager, he found a stash of science magazines. He studied them carefully. He learned that scientists were trying to make a new machine. It would use electricity to send and show pictures. He thought about it. He talked with his science teachers. One day he drew a picture on the chalkboard. It showed how a television could work. Philo Farnsworth's plan was the first idea that worked.

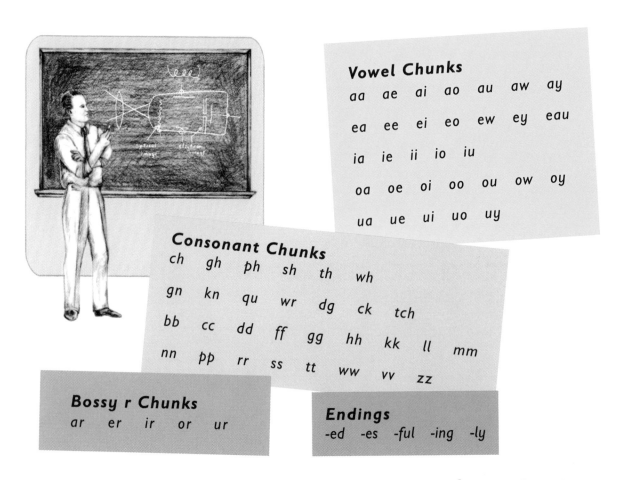

Vowel Chunks

aa   ae   ai   ao   au   aw   ay

ea   ee   ei   eo   ew   ey   eau

ia   ie   ii   io   iu

oa   oe   oi   oo   ou   ow   oy

ua   ue   ui   uo   uy

Consonant Chunks

ch   gh   ph   sh   th   wh

gn   kn   qu   wr   dg   ck   tch

bb   cc   dd   ff   gg   hh   kk   ll   mm

nn   pp   rr   ss   tt   ww   vv   zz

Bossy r Chunks

ar   er   ir   or   ur

Endings

-ed   -es   -ful   -ing   -ly

Copy and chunk the story.

It would use electricity to send

I

and show pictures. He thought

a

about it. He talked with his

a

science teachers. One day he drew

s

a picture on the chalkboard. It

a

showed how a television could

s

work. Philo Farnsworth's plan was

w

the first idea that worked.

t

1. Read the story to your student.

2. Read it together slowly, looking carefully at each word.

3. Have the student mark the **vowel chunks** (yellow), **consonant chunks** (blue), **Bossy _r_ chunks** (purple), **Tricky _y_ Guy** (green), **endings** (pink or red), and **silent letters** (orange).

Philo was very interested in electronics. When he was a teenager, he found a stash of science magazines. He studied them carefully. He learned that scientists were trying to make a new machine. It would use electricity to send and show pictures. He thought about it. He talked with his science teachers. One day he drew a picture on the chalkboard. It showed how a television could work. Philo Farnsworth's plan was the first idea that worked.

Vowel Chunks

aa ae ai ao au aw ay

ea ee ei eo ew ey eau

ia ie ii io iu

oa oe oi oo ou ow oy

ua ue ui uo uy

Consonant Chunks

ch gh ph sh th wh

gn kn qu wr dg ck tch

bb cc dd ff gg hh kk ll mm

nn pp rr ss tt ww vv zz

Bossy r Chunks

ar er ir or ur

Endings

-ed -es -ful -ing -ly

Copy and chunk the story.

Philo was very interested in

P

electronics. When he was a

e

teenager, he found a stash of

t

science magazines. He studied

s

them carefully. He learned that

t

scientists were trying to make a

s

new machine. It would use

n

electricity to send and show

e

pictures. He thought about it.

P

1. Read the story to your student.

2. Read it together slowly, looking carefully at each word.

3. Have the student mark the **vowel chunks** (yellow), **consonant chunks** (blue), **Bossy _r_ chunks** (purple), **Tricky _y_ Guy** (green), **endings** (pink or red), and **silent letters** (orange).

Philo was very interested in electronics. When he was a teenager, he found a stash of science magazines. He studied them carefully. He learned that scientists were trying to make a new machine. It would use electricity to send and show pictures. He thought about it. He talked with his science teachers. One day he drew a picture on the chalkboard. It showed how a television could work. Philo Farnsworth's plan was the first idea that worked.

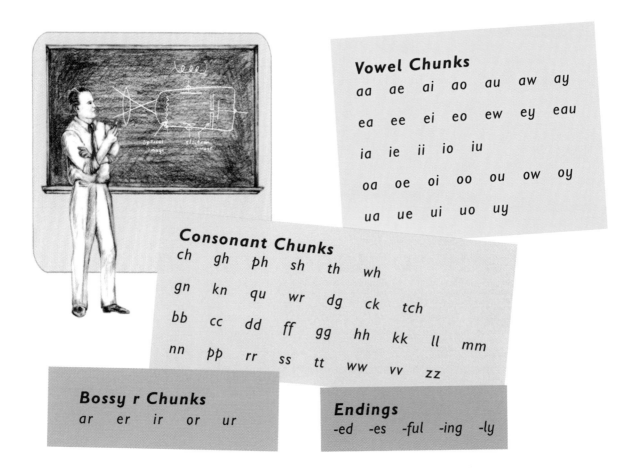

Vowel Chunks

aa ae ai ao au aw ay

ea ee ei eo ew ey eau

ia ie ii io iu

oa oe oi oo ou ow oy

ua ue ui uo uy

Consonant Chunks

ch gh ph sh th wh

gn kn qu wr dg ck tch

bb cc dd ff gg hh kk ll mm

nn pp rr ss tt ww vv zz

Bossy r Chunks

ar er ir or ur

Endings

-ed -es -ful -ing -ly

Write this week's story from dictation. Take your time and ask for help if you need it.

Philo

I spelled _____ words correctly.

1. Read the story to your student.

2. Read it together slowly, looking carefully at each word.

3. Have the student mark the **vowel chunks** (yellow), **consonant chunks** (blue), **Bossy _r_ chunks** (purple), **Tricky _y_ Guy** (green), **endings** (pink or red), and **silent letters** (orange).

Philo was very interested in electronics. When he was a teenager, he found a stash of science magazines. He studied them carefully. He learned that scientists were trying to make a new machine. It would use electricity to send and show pictures. He thought about it. He talked with his science teachers. One day he drew a picture on the chalkboard. It showed how a television could work. Philo Farnsworth's plan was the first idea that worked.

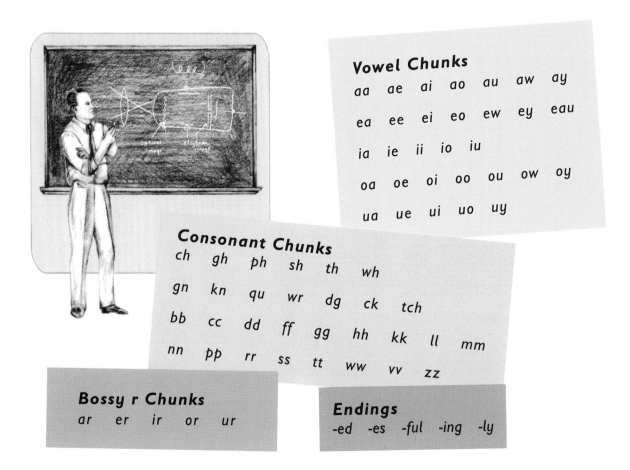

Vowel Chunks

aa ae ai ao au aw ay

ea ee ei eo ew ey eau

ia ie ii io iu

oa oe oi oo ou ow oy

ua ue ui uo uy

Consonant Chunks

ch gh ph sh th wh

gn kn qu wr dg ck tch

bb cc dd ff gg hh kk ll mm

nn pp rr ss tt ww vv zz

Bossy r Chunks

ar er ir or ur

Endings

-ed -es -ful -ing -ly

Section 2: Second Dictation

See if you can write this week's story from dictation without asking for help.

I spelled _____ words correctly.

1. Read the story to your student.

2. Read it together slowly, looking carefully at each word.

3. This week you and your student will be looking for and marking all six letter patterns that you have learned. They are <u>**vowel chunks**</u> (yellow), <u>**consonant chunks**</u> (blue), <u>**Bossy *r* chunks**</u> (purple), **Tricky *y* Guy** (green), <u>**endings**</u> (pink or red), and <u>**silent letters**</u> (orange).

America was scared of polio. It was a disease no one knew how to stop. Every summer more people became sick. Most were children. People with polio often couldn't use their legs anymore. Some couldn't breathe without a machine. Many died. Several scientists were asked to work on the problem. Jonas Salk was a doctor. His team worked long hours in a lab. Finally they discovered a safe vaccine. The whole country stopped to celebrate!

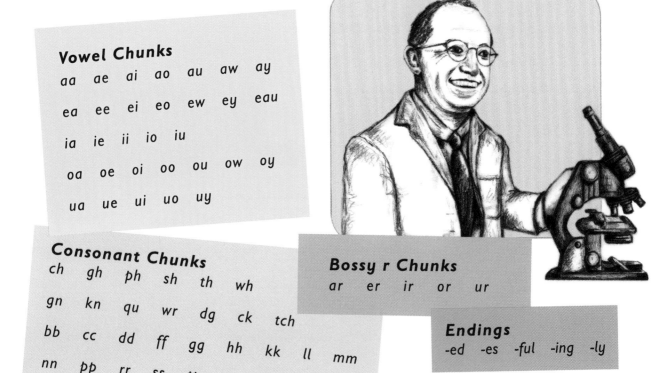

Vowel Chunks

aa ae ai ao au aw ay

ea ee ei eo ew ey eau

ia ie ii io iu

oa oe oi oo ou ow oy

ua ue ui uo uy

Consonant Chunks

ch gh ph sh th wh

gn kn qu wr dg ck tch

bb cc dd ff gg hh kk ll mm

nn pp rr ss tt ww vv zz

Bossy r Chunks

ar er ir or ur

Endings

-ed -es -ful -ing -ly

Copy and chunk the story.

America was scared of polio. It

A

was a disease no one knew how

w

to stop. Every summer more

t

people became sick. Most were

p

children. People with polio often

c

couldn't use their legs anymore.

c

Some couldn't breathe without a

S

machine. Many died.

m

1. Read the story to your student.

2. Read it together slowly, looking carefully at each word.

3. Have the student mark the **vowel chunks** (yellow), **consonant chunks** (blue), **Bossy *r* chunks** (purple), **Tricky *y* Guy** (green), **endings** (pink or red), and **silent letters** (orange).

America was scared of polio. It was a disease no one knew how to stop. Every summer more people became sick. Most were children. People with polio often couldn't use their legs anymore. Some couldn't breathe without a machine. Many died. Several scientists were asked to work on the problem. Jonas Salk was a doctor. His team worked long hours in a lab. Finally they discovered a safe vaccine. The whole country stopped to celebrate!

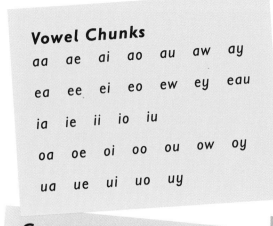

Vowel Chunks

aa ae ai ao au aw ay

ea ee ei eo ew ey eau

ia ie ii io iu

oa oe oi oo ou ow oy

ua ue ui uo uy

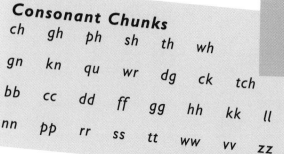

Consonant Chunks

ch gh ph sh th wh

gn kn qu wr dg ck tch

bb cc dd ff gg hh kk ll mm

nn pp rr ss tt ww vv zz

Bossy r Chunks

ar er ir or ur

Endings

-ed -es -ful -ing -ly

Copy and chunk the story.

Some couldn't breathe without a

S

machine. Many died. Several

m

scientists were asked to work on

s

the problem. Jonas Salk was a

t

doctor. His team worked long

d

hours in a lab. Finally they

h

discovered a safe vaccine. The

d

whole country stopped to

w

celebrate!

c

1. Read the story to your student.

2. Read it together slowly, looking carefully at each word.

3. Have the student mark the <u>**vowel chunks**</u> (yellow), <u>**consonant chunks**</u> (blue), <u>**Bossy *r* chunks**</u> (purple), <u>**Tricky *y* Guy**</u> (green), <u>**endings**</u> (pink or red), and <u>**silent letters**</u> (orange).

America was scared of polio. It was a disease no one knew how to stop. Every summer more people became sick. Most were children. People with polio often couldn't use their legs anymore. Some couldn't breathe without a machine. Many died. Several scientists were asked to work on the problem. Jonas Salk was a doctor. His team worked long hours in a lab. Finally they discovered a safe vaccine. The whole country stopped to celebrate!

Vowel Chunks
aa ae ai ao au aw ay
ea ee ei eo ew ey eau
ia ie ii io iu
oa oe oi oo ou ow oy
ua ue ui uo uy

Consonant Chunks
ch gh ph sh th wh
gn kn qu wr dg ck tch
bb cc dd ff gg hh kk ll mm
nn pp rr ss tt ww vv zz

Bossy r Chunks
ar er ir or ur

Endings
-ed -es -ful -ing -ly

Copy and chunk the story.

America was scared of polio. It

A

was a disease no one knew how

w

to stop. Every summer more

t

people became sick. Most were

p

children. People with polio often

c

couldn't use their legs anymore.

c

Some couldn't breathe without a

S

machine. Many died.

m

1. Read the story to your student.

2. Read it together slowly, looking carefully at each word.

3. Have the student mark the **vowel chunks** (yellow), **consonant chunks** (blue), **Bossy _r_ chunks** (purple), **Tricky _y_ Guy** (green), **endings** (pink or red), and **silent letters** (orange).

America was scared of polio. It was a disease no one knew how to stop. Every summer more people became sick. Most were children. People with polio often couldn't use their legs anymore. Some couldn't breathe without a machine. Many died. Several scientists were asked to work on the problem. Jonas Salk was a doctor. His team worked long hours in a lab. Finally they discovered a safe vaccine. The whole country stopped to celebrate!

Vowel Chunks

aa ae ai ao au aw ay

ea ee ei eo ew ey eau

ia ie ii io iu

oa oe oi oo ou ow oy

ua ue ui uo uy

Consonant Chunks

ch gh ph sh th wh

gn kn qu wr dg ck tch

bb cc dd ff gg hh kk ll mm

nn pp rr ss tt ww vv zz

Bossy r Chunks

ar er ir or ur

Endings

-ed -es -ful -ing -ly

Write this week's story from dictation. Take your time and ask for help if you need it.

America

I spelled _____ words correctly.

1. Read the story to your student.

2. Read it together slowly, looking carefully at each word.

3. Have the student mark the <u>**vowel chunks**</u> (yellow), <u>**consonant chunks**</u> (blue), <u>**Bossy *r* chunks**</u> (purple), <u>**Tricky *y* Guy**</u> (green), <u>**endings**</u> (pink or red), and <u>**silent letters**</u> (orange).

America was scared of polio. It was a disease no one knew how to stop. Every summer more people became sick. Most were children. People with polio often couldn't use their legs anymore. Some couldn't breathe without a machine. Many died. Several scientists were asked to work on the problem. Jonas Salk was a doctor. His team worked long hours in a lab. Finally they discovered a safe vaccine. The whole country stopped to celebrate!

Vowel Chunks

aa   ae   ai   ao   au   aw   ay

ea   ee   ei   eo   ew   ey   eau

ia   ie   ii   io   iu

oa   oe   oi   oo   ou   ow   oy

ua   ue   ui   uo   uy

Consonant Chunks

ch   gh   ph   sh   th   wh

gn   kn   qu   wr   dg   ck   tch

bb   cc   dd   ff   gg   hh   kk   ll   mm

nn   pp   rr   ss   tt   ww   vv   zz

Bossy r Chunks

ar   er   ir   or   ur

Endings

-ed   -es   -ful   -ing   -ly

Section 2: Second Dictation

See if you can write this week's story from dictation without asking for help.

I spelled _____ words correctly.

1. Read the story to your student.

2. Read it together slowly, looking carefully at each word.

3. This week you and your student will be looking for and marking all six letter patterns that you have learned. They are **vowel chunks** (yellow), **consonant chunks** (blue), **Bossy _r_ chunks** (purple), **Tricky _y_ Guy** (green), **endings** (pink or red), and **silent letters** (orange).

The Zamboni brothers built an indoor ice rink. It was very popular. There was one problem. As people skated, the ice became chipped and bumpy. Then four workers scraped the ice and wet it. It took an hour before people could skate again. Frank wanted to hurry the process. He invented a machine that did the same job in only fifteen minutes! It is still used on every ice rink today.

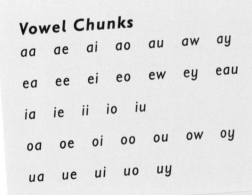

Vowel Chunks

aa ae ai ao au aw ay

ea ee ei eo ew ey eau

ia ie ii io iu

oa oe oi oo ou ow oy

ua ue ui uo uy

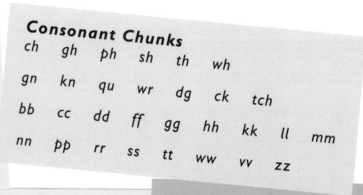

Consonant Chunks

ch gh ph sh th wh

gn kn qu wr dg ck tch

bb cc dd ff gg hh kk ll mm

nn pp rr ss tt ww vv zz

Bossy r Chunks

ar er ir or ur

Endings

-ed -es -ful -ing -ly

Copy and chunk the story.

The Zamboni brothers built an

T

indoor ice rink. It was very

i

popular. There was one problem.

P

As people skated, the ice became

A

chipped and bumpy. Then four

c

workers scraped the ice and wet

w

it. It took an hour before people

i

could skate again. Frank wanted

c

to hurry the process.

t

1. Read the story to your student.

2. Read it together slowly, looking carefully at each word.

3. Have the student mark the **vowel chunks** (yellow), **consonant chunks** (blue), **Bossy *r* chunks** (purple), **Tricky *y* Guy** (green), **endings** (pink or red), and **silent letters** (orange).

The Zamboni brothers built an indoor ice rink. It was very popular. There was one problem. As people skated, the ice became chipped and bumpy. Then four workers scraped the ice and wet it. It took an hour before people could skate again. Frank wanted to hurry the process. He invented a machine that did the same job in only fifteen minutes! It is still used on every ice rink today.

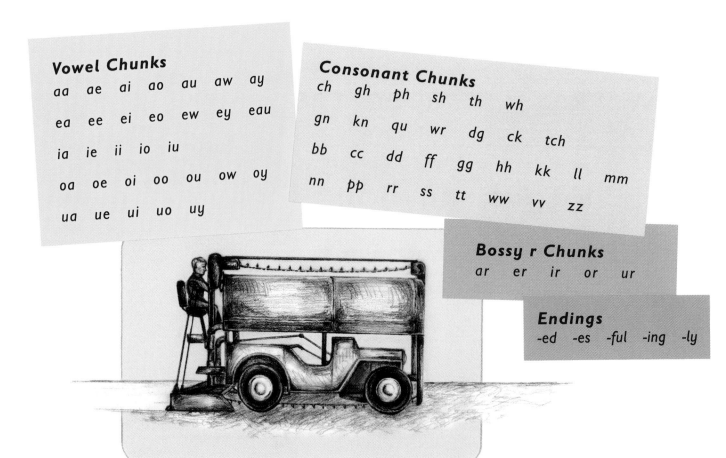

Vowel Chunks

aa	ae	ai	ao	au	aw	ay
ea	ee	ei	eo	ew	ey	eau
ia	ie	ii	io	iu		
oa	oe	oi	oo	ou	ow	oy
ua	ue	ui	uo	uy		

Consonant Chunks

ch	gh	ph	sh	th	wh	
gn	kn	qu	wr	dg	ck	tch
bb	cc	dd	ff	gg	hh	kk	ll	mm
nn	pp	rr	ss	tt	ww	vv	zz

Bossy r Chunks

ar   er   ir   or   ur

Endings

-ed   -es   -ful   -ing   -ly

Copy and chunk the story.

Then four workers scraped the

T

ice and wet it. It took an hour

i

before people could skate again.

b

Frank wanted to hurry the

F

process. He invented a machine

p

that did the same job in only

t

fifteen minutes! It is still used on

f

every ice rink today.

e

1. Read the story to your student.

2. Read it together slowly, looking carefully at each word.

3. Have the student mark the **vowel chunks** (yellow), **consonant chunks** (blue), **Bossy *r* chunks** (purple), **Tricky *y* Guy** (green), **endings** (pink or red), and **silent letters** (orange).

The Zamboni brothers built an indoor ice rink. It was very popular. There was one problem. As people skated, the ice became chipped and bumpy. Then four workers scraped the ice and wet it. It took an hour before people could skate again. Frank wanted to hurry the process. He invented a machine that did the same job in only fifteen minutes! It is still used on every ice rink today.

Vowel Chunks

aa	ae	ai	ao	au	aw	ay
ea	ee	ei	eo	ew	ey	eau
ia	ie	ii	io	iu		
oa	oe	oi	oo	ou	ow	oy
ua	ue	ui	uo	uy		

Consonant Chunks

ch	gh	ph	sh	th	wh	
gn	kn	qu	wr	dg	ck	tch
bb	cc	dd	ff	gg	hh	kk	ll	mm
nn	pp	rr	ss	tt	ww	vv	zz

Bossy r Chunks

ar   er   ir   or   ur

Endings

-ed   -es   -ful   -ing   -ly

Copy and chunk the story.

The Zamboni brothers built an

T

indoor ice rink. It was very

i

popular. There was one problem.

P

As people skated, the ice became

A

chipped and bumpy. Then four

c

workers scraped the ice and wet

w

it. It took an hour before people

i

could skate again. Frank wanted

c

to hurry the process.

t

1. Read the story to your student.

2. Read it together slowly, looking carefully at each word.

3. Have the student mark the **vowel chunks** (yellow), **consonant chunks** (blue), **Bossy _r_ chunks** (purple), **Tricky _y_ Guy** (green), **endings** (pink or red), and **silent letters** (orange).

The Zamboni brothers built an indoor ice rink. It was very popular. There was one problem. As people skated, the ice became chipped and bumpy. Then four workers scraped the ice and wet it. It took an hour before people could skate again. Frank wanted to hurry the process. He invented a machine that did the same job in only fifteen minutes! It is still used on every ice rink today.

Vowel Chunks

aa ae ai ao au aw ay

ea ee ei eo ew ey eau

ia ie ii io iu

oa oe oi oo ou ow oy

ua ue ui uo uy

Consonant Chunks

ch gh ph sh th wh

gn kn qu wr dg ck tch

bb cc dd ff gg hh kk ll mm

nn pp rr ss tt ww vv zz

Bossy r Chunks

ar er ir or ur

Endings

-ed -es -ful -ing -ly

Write this week's story from dictation. Take your time and ask for help if you need it.

The

I spelled _____ words correctly.

1. Read the story to your student.

2. Read it together slowly, looking carefully at each word.

3. Have the student mark the **vowel chunks** (yellow), **consonant chunks** (blue), **Bossy _r_ chunks** (purple), **Tricky _y_ Guy** (green), **endings** (pink or red), and **silent letters** (orange).

The Zamboni brothers built an indoor ice rink. It was very popular. There was one problem. As people skated, the ice became chipped and bumpy. Then four workers scraped the ice and wet it. It took an hour before people could skate again. Frank wanted to hurry the process. He invented a machine that did the same job in only fifteen minutes! It is still used on every ice rink today.

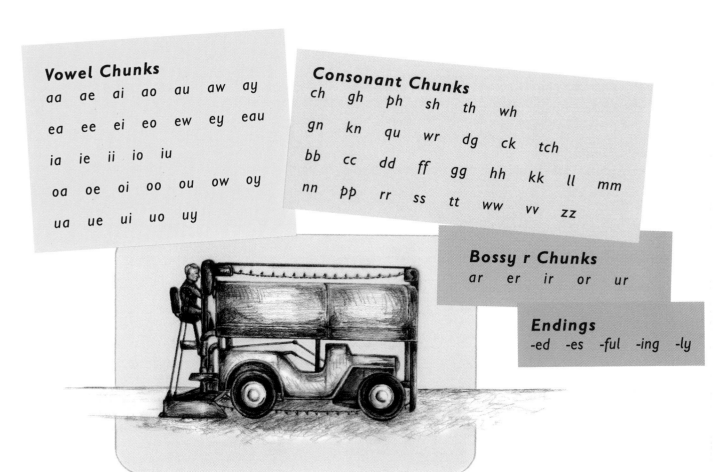

Vowel Chunks

aa ae ai ao au aw ay

ea ee ei eo ew ey eau

ia ie ii io iu

oa oe oi oo ou ow oy

ua ue ui uo uy

Consonant Chunks

ch gh ph sh th wh

gn kn qu wr dg ck tch

bb cc dd ff gg hh kk ll mm

nn pp rr ss tt ww vv zz

Bossy r Chunks

ar er ir or ur

Endings

-ed -es -ful -ing -ly

Section 2: Second Dictation

See if you can write this week's story from dictation without asking for help.

I spelled _____ words correctly.

1. Read the story to your student.

2. Read it together slowly, looking carefully at each word.

3. Have the student mark the <u>vowel chunks</u>, <u>consonant chunks</u>, <u>Bossy *r* chunks</u>, <u>Tricky *y* Guy</u>, <u>endings</u>, and <u>silent letters</u>, using the correct colors for each.

Dr. Silver did not know what to do with his new invention. He had been trying to make a strong glue. Instead, the glue he made was weak. He told the other workers about the new glue. He asked if they could think of any use for it. Arthur Fry listened. Later, Arthur went to choir practice. He was frustrated when the bookmarks in his music kept falling out. Suddenly he realized the new glue could be attached to paper, and the sticky note was born!

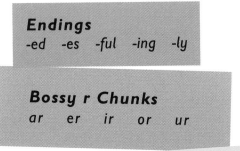

Endings
-ed   -es   -ful   -ing   -ly

Bossy r Chunks
ar   er   ir   or   ur

Vowel Chunks

aa	ae	ai	ao	au	aw	ay
ea	ee	ei	eo	ew	ey	eau
ia	ie	ii	io	iu		
oa	oe	oi	oo	ou	ow	oy
ua	ue	ui	uo	uy		

Consonant Chunks

ch	gh	ph	sh	th	wh			
gn	kn	qu	wr	dg	ck	tch		
bb	cc	dd	ff	gg	hh	kk	ll	mm
nn	pp	rr	ss	tt	ww	vv	zz	

Copy and chunk the story.

Dr. Silver did not know what to

D

do with his new invention. He had

d

been trying to make a strong glue.

b

Instead, the glue he made was

I

weak. He told the other workers

w

about the new glue. He asked if

a

they could think of any use for it.

t

Arthur Fry listened. Later, Arthur

A

went to choir practice.

w

1. Read the story to your student.

2. Read it together slowly, looking carefully at each word.

3. Have the student mark the <u>vowel chunks</u>, <u>consonant chunks</u>, <u>Bossy *r* chunks</u>, <u>Tricky *y* Guy</u>, <u>endings</u>, and <u>silent letters</u>, using the correct colors for each.

Dr. Silver did not know what to do with his new invention. He had been trying to make a strong glue. Instead, the glue he made was weak. He told the other workers about the new glue. He asked if they could think of any use for it. Arthur Fry listened. Later, Arthur went to choir practice. He was frustrated when the bookmarks in his music kept falling out. Suddenly he realized the new glue could be attached to paper, and the sticky note was born!

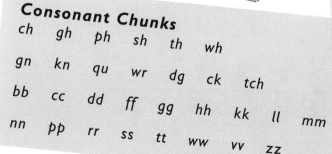

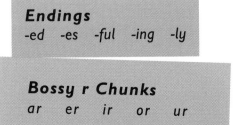

Endings
-ed -es -ful -ing -ly

Bossy r Chunks
ar   er   ir   or   ur

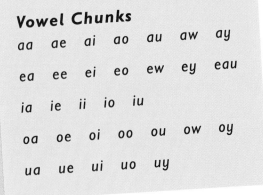

Vowel Chunks

aa	ae	ai	ao	au	aw	ay
ea	ee	ei	eo	ew	ey	eau
ia	ie	ii	io	iu		
oa	oe	oi	oo	ou	ow	oy
ua	ue	ui	uo	uy		

Consonant Chunks

ch	gh	ph	sh	th	wh		
gn	kn	qu	wr	dg	ck	tch	
bb	cc	dd	ff	gg	hh	kk	ll	mm
nn	pp	rr	ss	tt	ww	vv	zz

Section 2: Copywork

Copy and chunk the story.

He asked if they could think of

H

any use for it. Arthur Fry listened.

a

Later, Arthur went to choir

L

practice. He was frustrated when

P

the bookmarks in his music kept

t

falling out. Suddenly he realized

f

the new glue could be attached

t

to paper, and the sticky note

t

was born!

W

1. Read the story to your student.

2. Read it together slowly, looking carefully at each word.

3. Have the student mark the <u>**vowel chunks**</u>, <u>**consonant chunks**</u>, <u>**Bossy *r* chunks**</u>, <u>**Tricky *y* Guy**</u>, <u>**endings**</u>, and <u>**silent letters**</u>, using the correct colors for each.

Dr. Silver did not know what to do with his new invention. He had been trying to make a strong glue. Instead, the glue he made was weak. He told the other workers about the new glue. He asked if they could think of any use for it. Arthur Fry listened. Later, Arthur went to choir practice. He was frustrated when the bookmarks in his music kept falling out. Suddenly he realized the new glue could be attached to paper, and the sticky note was born!

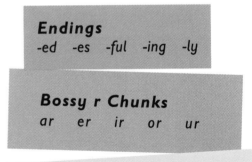

Endings
-ed   -es   -ful   -ing   -ly

Bossy r Chunks
ar   er   ir   or   ur

Vowel Chunks

aa	ae	ai	ao	au	aw	ay
ea	ee	ei	eo	ew	ey	eau
ia	ie	ii	io	iu		
oa	oe	oi	oo	ou	ow	oy
ua	ue	ui	uo	uy		

Consonant Chunks

ch	gh	ph	sh	th	wh		
gn	kn	qu	wr	dg	ck	tch	
bb	cc	dd	ff	gg	hh	kk	ll	mm
nn	pp	rr	ss	tt	ww	vv	zz

Copy and chunk the story.

Dr. Silver did not know what to

D

do with his new invention. He had

d

been trying to make a strong glue.

b

Instead, the glue he made was

I

weak. He told the other workers

w

about the new glue. He asked if

a

they could think of any use for it.

t

Arthur Fry listened. Later, Arthur

A

went to choir practice.

w

1. Read the story to your student.

2. Read it together slowly, looking carefully at each word.

3. Have the student mark the **vowel chunks**, **consonant chunks**, **Bossy _r_ chunks**, **Tricky _y_ Guy**, **endings**, and <u>**silent letters**</u>, using the correct colors for each.

Dr. Silver did not know what to do with his new invention. He had been trying to make a strong glue. Instead, the glue he made was weak. He told the other workers about the new glue. He asked if they could think of any use for it. Arthur Fry listened. Later, Arthur went to choir practice. He was frustrated when the bookmarks in his music kept falling out. Suddenly he realized the new glue could be attached to paper, and the sticky note was born!

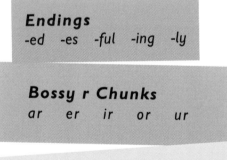

Endings
-ed   -es   -ful   -ing   -ly

Bossy r Chunks
ar   er   ir   or   ur

Vowel Chunks

aa	ae	ai	ao	au	aw	ay
ea	ee	ei	eo	ew	ey	eau
ia	ie	ii	io	iu		
oa	oe	oi	oo	ou	ow	oy
ua	ue	ui	uo	uy		

Consonant Chunks

ch	gh	ph	sh	th	wh				
gn	kn	qu	wr	dg	ck	tch			
bb	cc	dd	ff	gg	hh	kk	ll	mm	
nn	pp	rr	ss	tt	ww	vv	zz		

Section 2: First Dictation

Write this week's story from dictation. Take your time and ask for help if you need it.

Dr.

I spelled _____ words correctly. **131**

1. Read the story to your student.

2. Read it together slowly, looking carefully at each word.

3. Have the student mark the **vowel chunks**, **consonant chunks**, **Bossy _r_ chunks**, **Tricky _y_ Guy**, **endings**, and **silent letters**, using the correct colors for each.

Dr. Silver did not know what to do with his new invention. He had been trying to make a strong glue. Instead, the glue he made was weak. He told the other workers about the new glue. He asked if they could think of any use for it. Arthur Fry listened. Later, Arthur went to choir practice. He was frustrated when the bookmarks in his music kept falling out. Suddenly he realized the new glue could be attached to paper, and the sticky note was born!

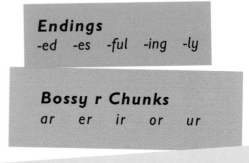

Endings
-ed -es -ful -ing -ly

Bossy r Chunks
ar   er   ir   or   ur

Vowel Chunks
aa ae ai ao au aw ay
ea ee ei eo ew ey eau
ia ie ii io iu
oa oe oi oo ou ow oy
ua ue ui uo uy

Consonant Chunks
ch gh ph sh th wh
gn kn qu wr dg ck tch
bb cc dd ff gg hh kk ll mm
nn pp rr ss tt ww vv zz

Section 2: Second Dictation

See if you can write this week's story from dictation without asking for help.

I spelled _____ words correctly.

32A

Section 1: All Letter Patterns

1. Read the story to your student.

2. Read it together slowly, looking carefully at each word.

3. Have the student mark the **vowel chunks**, **consonant chunks**, **Bossy _r_ chunks**, **Tricky _y_ Guy**, **endings**, and **silent letters**, using the correct colors for each.

A terrible accident happened at the schoolhouse! Glenn's legs were very badly burned. The doctors wanted to remove them. He told his parents he did not want that. Glenn worked very hard to get well. To the doctors' surprise, he started walking again. No one thought that some day he would run in the Olympics. Glenn Cunningham set a world record for the mile run!

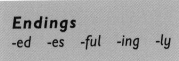

Endings
-ed   -es   -ful   -ing   -ly

Vowel Chunks

aa	ae	ai	ao	au	aw	ay
ea	ee	ei	eo	ew	ey	eau
ia	ie	ii	io	iu		
oa	oe	oi	oo	ou	ow	oy
ua	ue	ui	uo	uy		

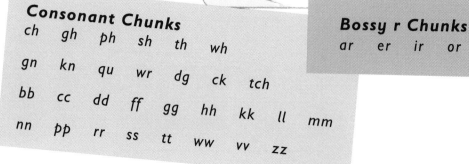

Consonant Chunks

ch	gh	ph	sh	th	wh	
gn	kn	qu	wr	dg	ck	tch
bb	cc	dd	ff	gg	hh	kk	ll	mm
nn	pp	rr	ss	tt	ww	vv	zz

Bossy r Chunks
ar   er   ir   or   ur

Copy and chunk the story.

A terrible accident happened at
A

the schoolhouse! Glenn's legs were
t

very badly burned. The doctors
v

wanted to remove them. He told
w

his parents he did not want that.
h

Glenn worked very hard to get
G

well. To the doctors' surprise, he
w

started walking again.
s

1. Read the story to your student.

2. Read it together slowly, looking carefully at each word.

3. Have the student mark the **vowel chunks**, **consonant chunks**, **Bossy _r_ chunks**, **Tricky _y_ Guy**, **endings**, and **silent letters**, using the correct colors for each.

A terrible accident happened at the schoolhouse! Glenn's legs were very badly burned. The doctors wanted to remove them. He told his parents he did not want that. Glenn worked very hard to get well. To the doctors' surprise, he started walking again. No one thought that some day he would run in the Olympics. Glenn Cunningham set a world record for the mile run!

Endings
-ed   -es   -ful   -ing   -ly

Vowel Chunks

aa	ae	ai	ao	au	aw	ay
ea	ee	ei	eo	ew	ey	eau
ia	ie	ii	io	iu		
oa	oe	oi	oo	ou	ow	oy
ua	ue	ui	uo	uy		

Consonant Chunks

ch	gh	ph	sh	th	wh			
gn	kn	qu	wr	dg	ck	tch		
bb	cc	dd	ff	gg	hh	kk	ll	mm
nn	pp	rr	ss	tt	ww	vv	zz	

Bossy r Chunks
ar   er   ir   or   ur

Copy and chunk the story.

The doctors wanted to remove

T

them. He told his parents he did

t

not want that. Glenn worked very

n

hard to get well. To the doctors'

h

surprise, he started walking again.

s

No one thought that some day he

N

would run in the Olympics. Glenn

w

Cunningham set a world record

C

for the mile run!

f

1. Read the story to your student.

2. Read it together slowly, looking carefully at each word.

3. Have the student mark the <u>vowel chunks</u>, <u>consonant chunks</u>, <u>**Bossy *r* chunks**</u>, Tricky *y* Guy, <u>endings</u>, and <u>silent letters</u>, using the correct colors for each.

A terrible accident happened at the schoolhouse! Glenn's legs were very badly burned. The doctors wanted to remove them. He told his parents he did not want that. Glenn worked very hard to get well. To the doctors' surprise, he started walking again. No one thought that some day he would run in the Olympics. Glenn Cunningham set a world record for the mile run!

Endings

-ed   -es   -ful   -ing   -ly

Vowel Chunks

aa	ae	ai	ao	au	aw	ay
ea	ee	ei	eo	ew	ey	eau
ia	ie	ii	io	iu
oa	oe	oi	oo	ou	ow	oy
ua	ue	ui	uo	uy

Consonant Chunks

ch	gh	ph	sh	th	wh
gn	kn	qu	wr	dg	ck	tch
bb	cc	dd	ff	gg	hh	kk	ll	mm
nn	pp	rr	ss	tt	ww	vv	zz

Bossy r Chunks

ar   er   ir   or   ur

Copy and chunk the story.

A terrible accident happened at

A

the schoolhouse! Glenn's legs were

t

very badly burned. The doctors

v

wanted to remove them. He told

w

his parents he did not want that.

h

Glenn worked very hard to get

G

well. To the doctors' surprise, he

w

started walking again.

s

32D

1. Read the story to your student.

2. Read it together slowly, looking carefully at each word.

3. Have the student mark the <u>vowel chunks</u>, <u>consonant chunks</u>, <u>Bossy *r* chunks</u>, <u>Tricky *y* Guy</u>, <u>endings</u>, and <u>silent letters</u>, using the correct colors for each.

A terrible accident happened at the schoolhouse! Glenn's legs were very badly burned. The doctors wanted to remove them. He told his parents he did not want that. Glenn worked very hard to get well. To the doctors' surprise, he started walking again. No one thought that some day he would run in the Olympics. Glenn Cunningham set a world record for the mile run!

Endings

-ed   -es   -ful   -ing   -ly

Vowel Chunks

aa   ae   ai   ao   au   aw   ay

ea   ee   ei   eo   ew   ey   eau

ia   ie   ii   io   iu

oa   oe   oi   oo   ou   ow   oy

ua   ue   ui   uo   uy

Consonant Chunks

ch   gh   ph   sh   th   wh

gn   kn   qu   wr   dg   ck   tch

bb   cc   dd   ff   gg   hh   kk   ll   mm

nn   pp   rr   ss   tt   ww   vv   zz

Bossy r Chunks

ar   er   ir   or   ur

Write this week's story from dictation. Take your time and ask for help if you need it.

A

I spelled _____ words correctly.

1. Read the story to your student.

2. Read it together slowly, looking carefully at each word.

3. Have the student mark the <u>**vowel chunks**</u>, <u>**consonant chunks**</u>, <u>**Bossy *r* chunks**</u>, **Tricky *y* Guy**, <u>**endings**</u>, and <u>**silent letters**</u>, using the correct colors for each.

A terrible accident happened at the schoolhouse! Glenn's legs were very badly burned. The doctors wanted to remove them. He told his parents he did not want that. Glenn worked very hard to get well. To the doctors' surprise, he started walking again. No one thought that some day he would run in the Olympics. Glenn Cunningham set a world record for the mile run!

Endings

-ed   -es   -ful   -ing   -ly

Vowel Chunks

aa   ae   ai   ao   au   aw   ay

ea   ee   ei   eo   ew   ey   eau

ia   ie   ii   io   iu

oa   oe   oi   oo   ou   ow   oy

ua   ue   ui   uo   uy

Consonant Chunks

ch   gh   ph   sh   th   wh

gn   kn   qu   wr   dg   ck   tch

bb   cc   dd   ff   gg   hh   kk   ll   mm

nn   pp   rr   ss   tt   ww   vv   zz

Bossy r Chunks

ar   er   ir   or   ur

See if you can write this week's story from dictation without asking for help.

1. Read the story to your student.

2. Read it together slowly, looking carefully at each word.

3. Have the student mark the **vowel chunks**, **consonant chunks**, **Bossy _r_ chunks**, **Tricky _y_ Guy**, **endings**, and **silent letters**, using the correct colors for each.

John D. Rockefeller was very wealthy. He gave away a lot of his money. He helped start several colleges. He started high schools for African Americans. He also cared about people's health. Hookworms were a big problem in the South. They made thousands of people ill. Being sick made it hard for children to learn. John started a program that helped get rid of hookworms. It made many lives better.

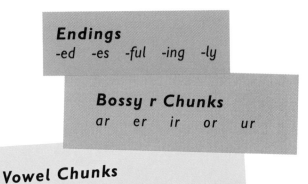

Endings

-ed   -es   -ful   -ing   -ly

Bossy r Chunks

ar   er   ir   or   ur

Vowel Chunks

aa	ae	ai	ao	au	aw	ay
ea	ee	ei	eo	ew	ey	eau
ia	ie	ii	io	iu		
oa	oe	oi	oo	ou	ow	oy
ua	ue	ui	uo	uy		

Consonant Chunks

ch	gh	ph	sh	th	wh	
gn	kn	qu	wr	dg	ck	tch
bb	cc	dd	ff	gg	hh	kk	ll	mm
nn	pp	rr	ss	tt	ww	vv	zz

Copy and chunk the story.

John D. Rockefeller was very

J

wealthy. He gave away a lot of

w

his money. He helped start several

h

colleges. He started high schools

c

for African Americans. He also

f

cared about people's health.

c

Hookworms were a big problem in

H

the South. They made thousands

t

of people ill.

o

1. Read the story to your student.

2. Read it together slowly, looking carefully at each word.

3. Have the student mark the <u>vowel chunks</u>, <u>consonant chunks</u>, <u>Bossy *r* chunks</u>, <u>Tricky *y* Guy</u>, <u>endings</u>, and <u>silent letters</u>, using the correct colors for each.

John D. Rockefeller was very wealthy. He gave away a lot of his money. He helped start several colleges. He started high schools for African Americans. He also cared about people's health. Hookworms were a big problem in the South. They made thousands of people ill. Being sick made it hard for children to learn. John started a program that helped get rid of hookworms. It made many lives better.

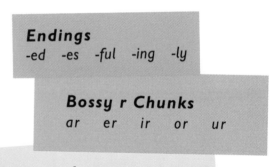

Endings
-ed   -es   -ful   -ing   -ly

Bossy r Chunks
ar   er   ir   or   ur

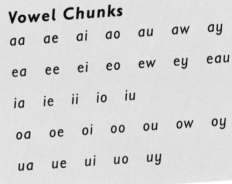

Vowel Chunks

aa ae ai ao au aw ay

ea ee ei eo ew ey eau

ia ie ii io iu

oa oe oi oo ou ow oy

ua ue ui uo uy

Consonant Chunks

ch gh ph sh th wh

gn kn qu wr dg ck tch

bb cc dd ff gg hh kk ll mm

nn pp rr ss tt ww vv zz

Copy and chunk the story.

He also cared about people's

H

health. Hookworms were a big

h

problem in the South. They made

p

thousands of people ill. Being sick

t

made it hard for children to learn.

m

John started a program that

J

helped get rid of hookworms. It

h

made many lives better.

m

1. Read the story to your student.

2. Read it together slowly, looking carefully at each word.

3. Have the student mark the <u>vowel chunks</u>, <u>consonant chunks</u>, <u>**Bossy** *r* **chunks**</u>, <u>**Tricky** *y* **Guy**</u>, <u>endings</u>, and <u>silent letters</u>, using the correct colors for each.

John D. Rockefeller was very wealthy. He gave away a lot of his money. He helped start several colleges. He started high schools for African Americans. He also cared about people's health. Hookworms were a big problem in the South. They made thousands of people ill. Being sick made it hard for children to learn. John started a program that helped get rid of hookworms. It made many lives better.

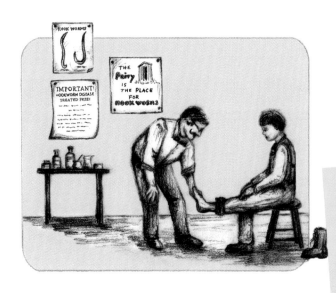

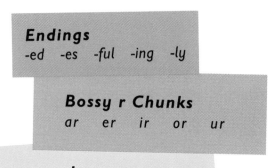

Endings

-ed   -es   -ful   -ing   -ly

Bossy r Chunks

ar   er   ir   or   ur

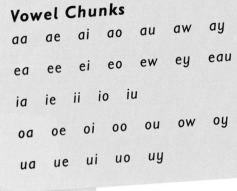

Vowel Chunks

aa	ae	ai	ao	au	aw	ay
ea	ee	ei	eo	ew	ey	eau
ia	ie	ii	io	iu		
oa	oe	oi	oo	ou	ow	oy
ua	ue	ui	uo	uy		

Consonant Chunks

ch	gh	ph	sh	th	wh			
gn	kn	qu	wr	dg	ck	tch		
bb	cc	dd	ff	gg	hh	kk	ll	mm
nn	pp	rr	ss	tt	ww	vv	zz	

Copy and chunk the story.

John D. Rockefeller was very

J

wealthy. He gave away a lot of

w

his money. He helped start several

h

colleges. He started high schools

c

for African Americans. He also

f

cared about people's health.

c

Hookworms were a big problem in

H

the South. They made thousands

t

of people ill.

o

1. Read the story to your student.

2. Read it together slowly, looking carefully at each word.

3. Have the student mark the **vowel chunks**, **consonant chunks**, **Bossy *r* chunks**, **Tricky *y* Guy**, **endings**, and **silent letters**, using the correct colors for each.

John D. Rockefeller was very wealthy. He gave away a lot of his money. He helped start several colleges. He started high schools for African Americans. He also cared about people's health. Hookworms were a big problem in the South. They made thousands of people ill. Being sick made it hard for children to learn. John started a program that helped get rid of hookworms. It made many lives better.

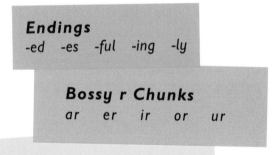

Endings
-ed   -es   -ful   -ing   -ly

Bossy r Chunks
ar   er   ir   or   ur

Vowel Chunks

aa	ae	ai	ao	au	aw	ay
ea	ee	ei	eo	ew	ey	eau
ia	ie	ii	io	iu		
oa	oe	oi	oo	ou	ow	oy
ua	ue	ui	uo	uy		

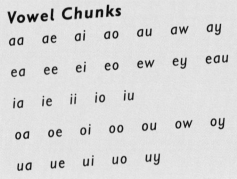

Consonant Chunks

ch	gh	ph	sh	th	wh		
gn	kn	qu	wr	dg	ck	tch	
bb	cc	dd	ff	gg	hh	kk	ll	mm
nn	pp	rr	ss	tt	ww	vv	zz

Write this week's story from dictation. Take your time and ask for help if you need it.

John

I spelled _____ words correctly.

1. Read the story to your student.

2. Read it together slowly, looking carefully at each word.

3. Have the student mark the <u>vowel chunks</u>, <u>consonant chunks</u>, <u>Bossy *r* chunks</u>, <u>Tricky *y* Guy</u>, <u>endings</u>, and <u>silent letters</u>, using the correct colors for each.

John D. Rockefeller was very wealthy. He gave away a lot of his money. He helped start several colleges. He started high schools for African Americans. He also cared about people's health. Hookworms were a big problem in the South. They made thousands of people ill. Being sick made it hard for children to learn. John started a program that helped get rid of hookworms. It made many lives better.

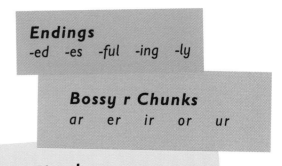

Endings
-ed   -es   -ful   -ing   -ly

Bossy r Chunks
ar   er   ir   or   ur

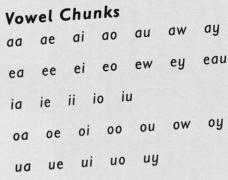

Vowel Chunks

aa   ae   ai   ao   au   aw   ay

ea   ee   ei   eo   ew   ey   eau

ia   ie   ii   io   iu

oa   oe   oi   oo   ou   ow   oy

ua   ue   ui   uo   uy

Consonant Chunks

ch   gh   ph   sh   th   wh

gn   kn   qu   wr   dg   ck   tch

bb   cc   dd   ff   gg   hh   kk   ll   mm

nn   pp   rr   ss   tt   ww   vv   zz

Section 2: Second Dictation

See if you can write this week's story from dictation without asking for help.

I spelled _____ words correctly.

1. Read the story to your student.

2. Read it together slowly, looking carefully at each word.

3. Have the student mark the **vowel chunks**, **consonant chunks**, **Bossy _r_ chunks**, **Tricky _y_ Guy**, **endings**, and **silent letters**, using the correct colors for each.

During World War 2, the whole country worked together.
Many American soldiers were fighting. They needed food and
clothing. People at home worked hard and saved. They could
use only a certain amount of meat and sugar. They could not
buy a lot of gasoline. Many women went to work. Factories
made tanks and planes instead of new cars. Even children
helped! They collected scrap metal and rubber.

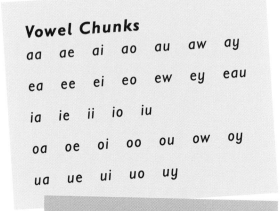

Vowel Chunks

aa ae ai ao au aw ay

ea ee ei eo ew ey eau

ia ie ii io iu

oa oe oi oo ou ow oy

ua ue ui uo uy

Bossy r Chunks

ar er ir or ur

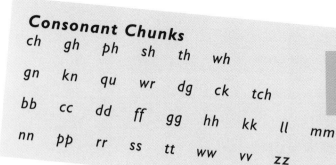

Consonant Chunks

ch gh ph sh th wh

gn kn qu wr dg ck tch

bb cc dd ff gg hh kk ll mm

nn pp rr ss tt ww vv zz

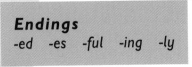

Endings

-ed -es -ful -ing -ly

Copy and chunk the story.

During World War 2, the whole

D

country worked together. Many

c

American soldiers were fighting.

A

They needed food and clothing.

T

People at home worked hard and

P

saved. They could use only a

s

certain amount of meat and sugar.

c

They could not buy a lot of

T

gasoline.

g

1. Read the story to your student.

2. Read it together slowly, looking carefully at each word.

3. Have the student mark the <u>vowel chunks</u>, <u>consonant chunks</u>, <u>Bossy *r* chunks</u>, <u>Tricky *y* Guy</u>, <u>endings</u>, and <u>silent letters</u>, using the correct colors for each.

During World War 2, the whole country worked together. Many American soldiers were fighting. They needed food and clothing. People at home worked hard and saved. They could use only a certain amount of meat and sugar. They could not buy a lot of gasoline. Many women went to work. Factories made tanks and planes instead of new cars. Even children helped! They collected scrap metal and rubber.

Vowel Chunks

aa ae ai ao au aw ay

ea ee ei eo ew ey eau

ia ie ii io iu

oa oe oi oo ou ow oy

ua ue ui uo uy

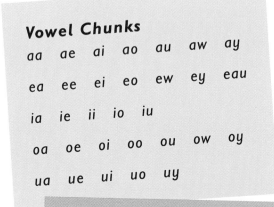

Bossy r Chunks

ar   er   ir   or   ur

Consonant Chunks

ch gh ph sh th wh

gn kn qu wr dg ck tch

bb cc dd ff gg hh kk ll mm

nn pp rr ss tt ww vv zz

Endings

-ed -es -ful -ing -ly

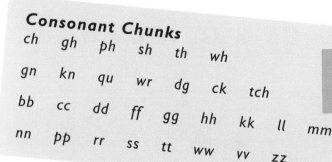

Copy and chunk the story.

People at home worked hard and

P

saved. They could use only a

s

certain amount of meat and sugar.

c

They could not buy a lot of

T

gasoline. Many women went to

g

work. Factories made tanks and

w

planes instead of new cars. Even

P

children helped! They collected

c

scrap metal and rubber.

s

1. Read the story to your student.

2. Read it together slowly, looking carefully at each word.

3. Have the student mark the **vowel chunks**, **consonant chunks**, **Bossy *r* chunks**, **Tricky *y* Guy**, **endings**, and **silent letters**, using the correct colors for each.

During World War 2, the whole country worked together. Many American soldiers were fighting. They needed food and clothing. People at home worked hard and saved. They could use only a certain amount of meat and sugar. They could not buy a lot of gasoline. Many women went to work. Factories made tanks and planes instead of new cars. Even children helped! They collected scrap metal and rubber.

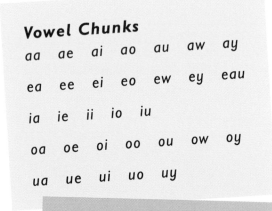

Vowel Chunks

aa	ae	ai	ao	au	aw	ay
ea	ee	ei	eo	ew	ey	eau
ia	ie	ii	io	iu		
oa	oe	oi	oo	ou	ow	oy
ua	ue	ui	uo	uy		

Bossy r Chunks

ar er ir or ur

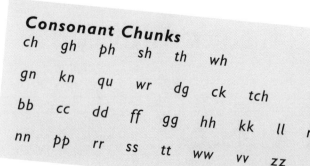

Consonant Chunks

ch	gh	ph	sh	th	wh
gn	kn	qu	wr	dg	ck	tch
bb	cc	dd	ff	gg	hh	kk	ll	mm
nn	pp	rr	ss	tt	ww	vv	zz

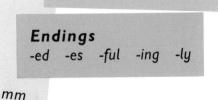

Endings

-ed -es -ful -ing -ly

Copy and chunk the story.

During World War 2, the whole

D

country worked together. Many

c

American soldiers were fighting.

A

They needed food and clothing.

T

People at home worked hard and

P

saved. They could use only a

s

certain amount of meat and sugar.

c

They could not buy a lot of

T

gasoline.

g

1. Read the story to your student.

2. Read it together slowly, looking carefully at each word.

3. Have the student mark the <u>vowel chunks</u>, <u>consonant chunks</u>, <u>Bossy *r* chunks</u>, <u>Tricky *y* Guy</u>, <u>endings</u>, and <u>silent letters</u>, using the correct colors for each.

During World War 2, the whole country worked together. Many American soldiers were fighting. They needed food and clothing. People at home worked hard and saved. They could use only a certain amount of meat and sugar. They could not buy a lot of gasoline. Many women went to work. Factories made tanks and planes instead of new cars. Even children helped! They collected scrap metal and rubber.

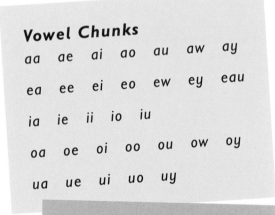

Vowel Chunks

aa	ae	ai	ao	au	aw	ay
ea	ee	ei	eo	ew	ey	eau
ia	ie	ii	io	iu		
oa	oe	oi	oo	ou	ow	oy
ua	ue	ui	uo	uy		

Bossy r Chunks

ar   er   ir   or   ur

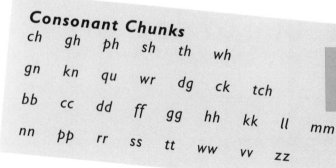

Consonant Chunks

ch	gh	ph	sh	th	wh			
gn	kn	qu	wr	dg	ck	tch		
bb	cc	dd	ff	gg	hh	kk	ll	mm
nn	pp	rr	ss	tt	ww	vv	zz	

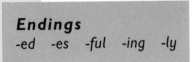

Endings

-ed   -es   -ful   -ing   -ly

Write this week's story from dictation. Take your time and ask for help if you need it.

During

34E

1. Read the story to your student.

2. Read it together slowly, looking carefully at each word.

3. Have the student mark the **vowel chunks**, **consonant chunks**, **Bossy _r_ chunks**, Tricky _y_ Guy, **endings**, and **silent letters**, using the correct colors for each.

During World War 2, the whole country worked together. Many American soldiers were fighting. They needed food and clothing. People at home worked hard and saved. They could use only a certain amount of meat and sugar. They could not buy a lot of gasoline. Many women went to work. Factories made tanks and planes instead of new cars. Even children helped! They collected scrap metal and rubber.

Vowel Chunks

aa ae ai ao au aw ay

ea ee ei eo ew ey eau

ia ie ii io iu

oa oe oi oo ou ow oy

ua ue ui uo uy

Bossy r Chunks

ar   er   ir   or   ur

Consonant Chunks

ch gh ph sh th wh

gn kn qu wr dg ck tch

bb cc dd ff gg hh kk ll mm

nn pp rr ss tt ww vv zz

Endings

-ed -es -ful -ing -ly

Section 2: Second Dictation

See if you can write this week's story from dictation without asking for help.

I spelled _____ words correctly. **163**

1. Read the story to your student.

2. Read it together slowly, looking carefully at each word.

3. Have the student mark the <u>vowel chunks</u>, <u>consonant chunks</u>, <u>**Bossy** *r* **chunks**</u>, <u>**Tricky** *y* **Guy**</u>, <u>endings</u>, and <u>silent letters</u>, using the correct colors for each.

In the 1950s, more people were driving cars and trucks. Busy roads went through every town. The army needed a way to get supplies from one place to another. A new highway system was built to solve these problems. These new roads had only a few places to get on and off. They went over or under all the old roads. Today, people use these highways to drive all over the country.

Bossy r Chunks
ar   er   ir   or   ur

Vowel Chunks
aa ae ai ao au aw ay
ea ee ei eo ew ey eau
ia ie ii io iu
oa oe oi oo ou ow oy
ua ue ui uo uy

Consonant Chunks
ch gh ph sh th wh
gn kn qu wr dg ck tch
bb cc dd ff gg hh kk ll mm
nn pp rr ss tt ww vv zz

Endings
-ed -es -ful -ing -ly

Section 1: All Letter Patterns

Copy and chunk the story.

In the 1950s, more people were

I

driving cars and trucks. Busy

d

roads went through every town.

r

The army needed a way to get

T

supplies from one place to another.

s

A new highway system was built

A

to solve these problems. These

t

new roads had only a few places

n

to get on and off.

t

35B

1. Read the story to your student.

2. Read it together slowly, looking carefully at each word.

3. Have the student mark the **vowel chunks**, **consonant chunks**, **Bossy *r* chunks**, **Tricky *y* Guy**, **endings**, and **silent letters**, using the correct colors for each.

In the 1950s, more people were driving cars and trucks. Busy roads went through every town. The army needed a way to get supplies from one place to another. A new highway system was built to solve these problems. These new roads had only a few places to get on and off. They went over or under all the old roads. Today, people use these highways to drive all over the country.

Bossy r Chunks

ar   er   ir   or   ur

Vowel Chunks

aa ae ai ao au aw ay

ea ee ei eo ew ey eau

ia ie ii io iu

oa oe oi oo ou ow oy

ua ue ui uo uy

Consonant Chunks

ch   gh   ph   sh   th   wh

gn   kn   qu   wr   dg   ck   tch

bb   cc   dd   ff   gg   hh   kk   ll   mm

nn   pp   rr   ss   tt   ww   vv   zz

Endings

-ed -es -ful -ing -ly

Copy and chunk the story.

The army needed a way to get

T

supplies from one place to another.

s

A new highway system was built

A

to solve these problems. These new

t

roads had only a few places to

r

get on and off. They went over or

g

under all the old roads. Today,

u

people use these highways to drive

p

all over the country.

a

1. Read the story to your student.

2. Read it together slowly, looking carefully at each word.

3. Have the student mark the **vowel chunks**, **consonant chunks**, **Bossy *r* chunks**, **Tricky *y* Guy**, **endings**, and **silent letters**, using the correct colors for each.

In the 1950s, more people were driving cars and trucks. Busy roads went through every town. The army needed a way to get supplies from one place to another. A new highway system was built to solve these problems. These new roads had only a few places to get on and off. They went over or under all the old roads. Today, people use these highways to drive all over the country.

Bossy r Chunks

ar   er   ir   or   ur

Vowel Chunks

aa   ae   ai   ao   au   aw   ay

ea   ee   ei   eo   ew   ey   eau

ia   ie   ii   io   iu

oa   oe   oi   oo   ou   ow   oy

ua   ue   ui   uo   uy

Consonant Chunks

ch   gh   ph   sh   th   wh

gn   kn   qu   wr   dg   ck   tch

bb   cc   dd   ff   gg   hh   kk   ll   mm

nn   pp   rr   ss   tt   ww   vv   zz

Endings

-ed   -es   -ful   -ing   -ly

Copy and chunk the story.

In the 1950s, more people were

I

driving cars and trucks. Busy

d

roads went through every town.

r

The army needed a way to get

T

supplies from one place to another.

s

A new highway system was built

A

to solve these problems. These

t

new roads had only a few places

n

to get on and off.

t

35D
Section 1: All Letter Patterns

1. Read the story to your student.

2. Read it together slowly, looking carefully at each word.

3. Have the student mark the **vowel chunks**, **consonant chunks**, **Bossy *r* chunks**, **Tricky *y* Guy**, **endings**, and **silent letters**, using the correct colors for each.

In the 1950s, more people were driving cars and trucks. Busy roads went through every town. The army needed a way to get supplies from one place to another. A new highway system was built to solve these problems. These new roads had only a few places to get on and off. They went over or under all the old roads. Today, people use these highways to drive all over the country.

Bossy r Chunks
ar   er   ir   or   ur

Vowel Chunks
aa ae ai ao au aw ay
ea ee ei eo ew ey eau
ia ie ii io iu
oa oe oi oo ou ow oy
ua ue ui uo uy

Consonant Chunks
ch gh ph sh th wh
gn kn qu wr dg ck tch
bb cc dd ff gg hh kk ll mm
nn pp rr ss tt ww vv zz

Endings
-ed -es -ful -ing -ly

Write this week's story from dictation. Take your time and ask for help if you need it.

In

I spelled _____ words correctly.

35E

1. Read the story to your student.

2. Read it together slowly, looking carefully at each word.

3. Have the student mark the **vowel chunks**, **consonant chunks**, **Bossy _r_ chunks**, **Tricky _y_ Guy**, **endings**, and **silent letters**, using the correct colors for each.

In the 1950s, more people were driving cars and trucks. Busy roads went through every town. The army needed a way to get supplies from one place to another. A new highway system was built to solve these problems. These new roads had only a few places to get on and off. They went over or under all the old roads. Today, people use these highways to drive all over the country.

Bossy r Chunks
ar   er   ir   or   ur

Vowel Chunks
aa   ae   ai   ao   au   aw   ay

ea   ee   ei   eo   ew   ey   eau

ia   ie   ii   io   iu

oa   oe   oi   oo   ou   ow   oy

ua   ue   ui   uo   uy

Consonant Chunks
ch   gh   ph   sh   th   wh

gn   kn   qu   wr   dg   ck   tch

bb   cc   dd   ff   gg   hh   kk   ll   mm

nn   pp   rr   ss   tt   ww   vv   zz

Endings
-ed   -es   -ful   -ing   -ly

Section 2: Second Dictation

See if you can write this week's story from dictation without asking for help.

I spelled _____ words correctly. **173**

36A

Section 1: All Letter Patterns

1. Read the story to your student.

2. Read it together slowly, looking carefully at each word.

3. Have the student mark the **vowel chunks**, **consonant chunks**, **Bossy *r* chunks**, **Tricky *y* Guy**, **endings**, and **silent letters**, using the correct colors for each.

Part of the American spirit is giving to others in need. To raise money we have bake sales and car washes. We go to special concerts. We plan sports events like races. We also collect food for the hungry. We donate clothing to homeless shelters. We give money to scientists to find cures for diseases. We help each other after storms and earthquakes. What could you do to help others?

Endings
-ed   -es   -ful   -ing   -ly

Bossy r Chunks
ar   er   ir   or   ur

Vowel Chunks
aa	ae	ai	ao	au	aw	ay
ea	ee	ei	eo	ew	ey	eau
ia	ie	ii	io	iu		
oa	oe	oi	oo	ou	ow	oy
ua	ue	ui	uo	uy		

Consonant Chunks
ch	gh	ph	sh	th	wh			
gn	kn	qu	wr	dg	ck	tch		
bb	cc	dd	ff	gg	hh	kk	ll	mm
nn	pp	rr	ss	tt	ww	vv	zz	

American Spirit Student

Section 2: Copywork

Copy and chunk the story.

Part of the American spirit is

P

giving to others in need. To raise

g

money we have bake sales and car

m

washes. We go to special concerts.

w

We plan sports events like races.

W

We also collect food for the

W

hungry. We donate clothing to

h

homeless shelters.

h

1. Read the story to your student.

2. Read it together slowly, looking carefully at each word.

3. Have the student mark the <u>**vowel chunks**</u>, <u>**consonant chunks**</u>, <u>**Bossy r chunks**</u>, <u>**Tricky y Guy**</u>, <u>**endings**</u>, and <u>**silent letters**</u>, using the correct colors for each.

Part of the American spirit is giving to others in need. To raise money we have bake sales and car washes. We go to special concerts. We plan sports events like races. We also collect food for the hungry. We donate clothing to homeless shelters. We give money to scientists to find cures for diseases. We help each other after storms and earthquakes. What could you do to help others?

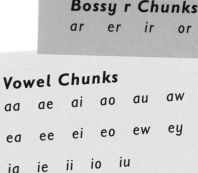

Endings
-ed   -es   -ful   -ing   -ly

Bossy r Chunks
ar   er   ir   or   ur

Vowel Chunks
aa   ae   ai   ao   au   aw   ay
ea   ee   ei   eo   ew   ey   eau
ia   ie   ii   io   iu
oa   oe   oi   oo   ou   ow   oy
ua   ue   ui   uo   uy

Consonant Chunks
ch   gh   ph   sh   th   wh
gn   kn   qu   wr   dg   ck   tch
bb   cc   dd   ff   gg   hh   kk   ll   mm
nn   pp   rr   ss   tt   ww   vv   zz

Section 2: Copywork

Copy and chunk the story.

We go to special concerts. We

W

plan sports events like races. We

p

also collect food for the hungry.

a

We donate clothing to homeless

W

shelters. We give money to

s

scientists to find cures for diseases.

s

We help each other after storms

W

and earthquakes. What could you

a

do to help others?

d

1. Read the story to your student.

2. Read it together slowly, looking carefully at each word.

3. Have the student mark the <u>vowel chunks</u>, <u>consonant chunks</u>, <u>Bossy *r* chunks</u>, <u>Tricky *y* Guy</u>, <u>endings</u>, and <u>silent letters</u>, using the correct colors for each.

Part of the American spirit is giving to others in need. To raise money we have bake sales and car washes. We go to special concerts. We plan sports events like races. We also collect food for the hungry. We donate clothing to homeless shelters. We give money to scientists to find cures for diseases. We help each other after storms and earthquakes. What could you do to help others?

Endings
-ed   -es   -ful   -ing   -ly

Bossy r Chunks
ar   er   ir   or   ur

Vowel Chunks

aa ae ai ao au aw ay

ea ee ei eo ew ey eau

ia ie ii io iu

oa oe oi oo ou ow oy

ua ue ui uo uy

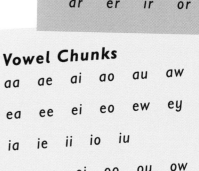

Consonant Chunks

ch gh ph sh th wh

gn kn qu wr dg ck tch

bb cc dd ff gg hh kk ll mm

nn pp rr ss tt ww vv zz

Copy and chunk the story.

Part of the American spirit is

P

giving to others in need. To raise

g

money we have bake sales and car

m

washes. We go to special concerts.

W

We plan sports events like races.

W

We also collect food for the

W

hungry. We donate clothing to

h

homeless shelters.

h

36D

Section 1: All Letter Patterns

1. Read the story to your student.

2. Read it together slowly, looking carefully at each word.

3. Have the student mark the <u>vowel chunks</u>, <u>consonant chunks</u>, <u>Bossy *r* chunks</u>, **Tricky *y* Guy**, <u>endings</u>, and <u>silent letters</u>, using the correct colors for each.

Part of the American spirit is giving to others in need. To raise money we have bake sales and car washes. We go to special concerts. We plan sports events like races. We also collect food for the hungry. We donate clothing to homeless shelters. We give money to scientists to find cures for diseases. We help each other after storms and earthquakes. What could you do to help others?

Endings

-ed -es -ful -ing -ly

Bossy r Chunks

ar   er   ir   or   ur

Vowel Chunks

aa ae ai ao au aw ay
ea ee ei eo ew ey eau
ia ie ii io iu
oa oe oi oo ou ow oy
ua ue ui uo uy

Consonant Chunks

ch gh ph sh th wh
gn kn qu wr dg ck tch
bb cc dd ff gg hh kk ll mm
nn pp rr ss tt ww vv zz

American Spirit Student

Write this week's story from dictation. Take your time and ask for help if you need it.

Part

1. Read the story to your student.

2. Read it together slowly, looking carefully at each word.

3. Have the student mark the **vowel chunks**, **consonant chunks**, **Bossy _r_ chunks**, **Tricky _y_ Guy**, **endings**, and **silent letters**, using the correct colors for each.

Part of the American spirit is giving to others in need. To raise money we have bake sales and car washes. We go to special concerts. We plan sports events like races. We also collect food for the hungry. We donate clothing to homeless shelters. We give money to scientists to find cures for diseases. We help each other after storms and earthquakes. What could you do to help others?

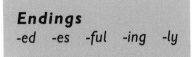

Endings
-ed -es -ful -ing -ly

Bossy r Chunks
ar   er   ir   or   ur

Vowel Chunks
aa ae ai ao au aw ay
ea ee ei eo ew ey eau
ia ie ii io iu
oa oe oi oo ou ow oy
ua ue ui uo uy

Consonant Chunks
ch gh ph sh th wh
gn kn qu wr dg ck tch
bb cc dd ff gg hh kk ll mm
nn pp rr ss tt ww vv zz

Section 2: Second Dictation

See if you can write this week's story from dictation without asking for help.